Effective
Financial
Management

THE SUNDAY TIMES

Effective Financial Management

Brian Finch

KoganPage

LONDON PHILADELPHIA NEW DELHI

Publisher's note

Every possible effort has been made to ensure that the information contained in this book is accurate at the time of going to press, and the publishers and authors cannot accept responsibility for any errors or omissions, however caused. No responsibility for loss or damage occasioned to any person acting, or refraining from action, as a result of the material in this publication can be accepted by the editor, the publisher or any of the authors.

First published in Great Britain and the United States in 2010 by Kogan Page Limited

120 Pentonville Road	525 South 4th Street, #241	4737/23 Ansari Road
London NI 9JN	Philadelphia PA 19147	Daryaganj
United Kingdom	USA	New Delhi 110002
www.koganpage.com		India

© Brian Finch, 2010

ISBN   978 0 7494 5878 2
E-ISBN 978 0 7494 5916 1

The views expressed in this book are those of the author, and are not necessarily the same as those of Times Newspapers Ltd.

British Library Cataloguing-in-Publication Data

A CIP record for this book is available from the British Library.

Library of Congress Cataloging-in-Publication Data

Finch, Brian.
    Effective financial management / Briain Finch.
        p. cm.
    ISBN 978-0-7494-5878-2 -- ISBN 978-0-7494-5916-1 (ebook) 1.
Business enterprise--Finance. I. Title.
    HG4026.F518 2010
    658.15--dc22

                                                                    2009036752

Typeset by Jean Cussons Typesetting, Diss, Norfolk
Printed and bound in India by Replika Press Pvt Ltd

Contents

Introduction

Effective financial management comprises more than accounting and reporting. It starts with raising money for a business, continues through maintaining investor relationships, includes accounting, reporting and communicating effectively with a wide range of stakeholders, involves budgeting, forecasting and managing business costs and cash flow, and assessing projects and buying assets. It covers selling a business too but that is a step too far for just one book.

The finance function in any business therefore has a role in the management and communication of everything involving money. In many businesses with smaller head offices it is also assigned responsibility for computer systems, facilities management, the company secretarial role and human resources issues. Since these really are separate functions I have only covered them peripherally, to the extent that all business processes are interlinked and must occasionally intrude into one another's territory.

Financial management is crucial at all stages in the business cycle and whatever the state of the business. Trade is generally easier when economies are growing but doing business in hard times provides extra opportunities as well as presenting particular problems. The opportunities arise from suppliers' willingness to reduce prices to maintain volume, and from acquisition opportunities being greater and the prices lower. It may be easier to acquire a business, premises or machinery from an administrator or liquidator at a much lower price or on more favourable credit terms than would have been possible before, but everyone is also fighting harder for a shrinking pie. During downturns it is not surprising if markets, processes and innovation actually evolve at a faster not a slower rate. It is a time to seek new ideas with even more vigour; to scour the trade press and the internet for hints of new products and services.

To offset these opportunities, bank finance will be harder to obtain. Banks will seek greater security and will value assets more harshly for security purposes. Credit generally will become more difficult to obtain. As part of this phenomenon, customers try to delay payment to improve their cash flow and pass to their suppliers a greater risk of incurring bad debts if they fail; whilst one business failing may have a knock-on effect with others either failing or having less cash available.

Effective financial management treats good times and bad equally but errs on the side of caution. This book starts with issues related to planning, goes through cost, asset and cash management to relationships with banks, landlords and the government. Inevitably some issues don't fit neatly into the flow and I have dealt with relationships with suppliers as a part of cash and cost management.

1

The business plan

The business plan is your tool for managing your business in good times and in bad as well as for a range of other needs such as raising finance, dealing with business partners and selling a business.

It focuses ideas; it helps you to examine what is not working and what is; it highlights areas of disagreement and allows these to be resolved; it provides a framework for putting numbers to ideas to test if they work and, if done well, it may even come up with new insights.

Review your planning team

Before writing a new business plan or revising an old one, think about who is to assemble this plan not just who will physically write it but who will provide the vision and the insights that are its backbone. Normally there will be several people involved in this process, except in the very smallest organisations.

If the business already exists and trades, the first thing to think about is how decisions are being made. Have we made good decisions or bad ones and if they are bad is there anything wrong with the way we made them? Successful businesses do not have dysfunctional management or team relationships at the top, whilst the main cause of failure is just that. So start by thinking about the business organisation, which should influence the composition of the planning team. There should be someone who is comfortable with financial issues involved but the process should not be driven by the finance function. Planning is not an extension of budgeting: it is about ideas and actions to achieve the organisation's vision.

Revise your business plan

What – the house is on fire and you want me to plan an extension? Yes, now's the time! Now is the moment to make time to look again at whatever you do and to ask if your goals and ambitions are appropriate and whether your strategies for attaining them are viable. Now is the time to completely reengineer what you do and to find a better way of doing it or even to do different things completely. Are there other ways to sell or to supply? Are there different products and services that fit your skills? What are your skills? Are you using the internet effectively? Are there opportunities through the social networking sites or through Twitter? Get out there and talk to people. Use networking organisations, try local Business Link networking events – they are often free. Go to trade shows, read the trade press and tune in to the blogs. On the web search engine Google you will find an option for blog search; but look at any blogs relating to your industry. The software nowadays enables you to keep a search live on key words so that if any blogs are posted on a subject that interests you, you will be informed instantly.

The directors of businesses should write down their thoughts in a formal business plan: it focuses minds on contradictions or problems in informal plans and leads to their resolution; it highlights differences of opinion that can be resolved; it results in objectives and strategies that can help everyone to rally around, be committed to and work towards. It may also be useful to show the plan to business partners or to submit it to banks to raise finance. If trading is tough it is a lot harder to convince banks to lend, which argues for having a better business plan.

Trading results

Before getting on to ideas, strategies and opportunities, demonstrate how your business has performed up until now. Show the last three years' figures and the forecast for the current year. It does not matter whether the reader is you or a bank manager – show the context because that will ensure that you are not unrealistic in your expectations and, if necessary, it will make your case convincing. If the figures tell a negative story, perhaps your business has just pottered along for the past few years and is hurting badly now; there is no reason to try to hide it. On the contrary, it forms a background for you to say, 'Right, we are making these changes that will alter our future ...'. Even if you are only outlining a survival strategy and have nothing more exciting to say than that you will cut costs, it needs a context.

Show your forecast figures on the same grid as the past trading. This will highlight changes and what needs to be explained in the body of the plan. I don't think that you need to show past budget figures in this grid – this would only reveal how good you have been at forecasting in the past but at the expense of making the table hard to read. A financier or investor may ask for this information but you should wait to be asked.

Use ratios

There are a number of ratios, described below, that are very helpful in analysing business performance. They should be used not just for the business plan but as a regular management tool; applied consistently and compared each month they will give early warning of things going both right and wrong. Ratio analysis poses questions; it does not give simple answers.

Gross margin

This is the sales figure, net of any sales taxes, less the cost of sales, divided by the net sales. The cost of sales is the variable cost of getting goods to the point of sale and it differs from industry to industry. In a retail environment it will be the cost of the stocks that are included in the sales figure; in a manufacturing business it will be the cost of materials used plus the direct cost of labour to get it to the finished condition plus a share of production overheads associated with that labour.

The gross margin calculation focuses attention on questions such as, 'Are we charging enough?' 'Are there products in the mix that we should not be selling?' 'Are our costs rising too much?'

Debtor days

This is the value of outstanding trade debtors divided by net annual sales and multiplied by 365 days. It shows, on average, how quickly customers are paying. Clearly there is a measure of seasonality in this and you could try to correct for this, perhaps by taking sales over a shorter period and multiplying by that number of days, not 365. I tend to think that, in most circumstances, that is probably over-sophistication: this ratio just gives a quick idea and if it is misleading just explain why and move on.

What you are looking for is an increase in the time customers take to pay that looks like a trend. It would suggest a need to investigate why; maybe less effective debtor control, a single big customer taking longer to pay, or the time of year.

Creditor days

This is the value of outstanding trade creditors divided by annual cost of sales and multiplied by 365 days.

Why should you care how long you are taking to pay your bills? Because if you are taking longer to pay that could show that you are running short of cash; or it could just be clever cash management. Ratios pose questions rather than giving answers.

Why is it restricted to trade creditors? Because you don't usually have much discretion over when you pay utility bills and the like, so including these distorts the picture. Also such costs are usually not included in the cost of sales.

Stock turn

This is the value of stocks at cost divided by the annual cost of sales and multiplied by 365 days. It excludes the profit margin because profit is not included in the value of stocks in the accounts. It is a measure of how much cash is tied up and can signal ageing stocks that are becoming hard to sell.

Gearing

This is the net debt (that is debt less cash in hand) the business has, divided by the aggregate of that debt plus shareholders' funds. An alternative version of the calculation divides debt by shareholders' funds alone. Gearing (also referred to as 'leverage') tracks how much debt (including bank loans, leasing, hire purchase and any debt factoring) the business has and can indicate shortage of cash if it is on a rising trend, and the level of risk in a business. The higher the gearing the greater the financial risk to the business but also the higher the proportionate rewards to equity when trade is buoyant. Its effects are similar to those illustrated below for operational gearing.

Other measures

Labour, overheads and, for some businesses, property occupation costs as a percentage of sales can all give a useful feel for trends. Clearly a well run business wants to show falling percentage labour, overhead and property costs together with rising margins.

Operational gearing

This expresses the effect of the ratio of fixed to variable costs in a business. There are a number of slightly different ratios that all, effectively, do the same job. The simplest method is to calculate the ratio of fixed costs to sales. Higher operational gearing means that a business responds proportionately better to increasing sales and worse to declining sales, as illustrated in Tables 1.1 to 1.3.

Table 1.1

	Company A	Company B
Sales	1,000	1,000
Variable costs	700	800
Fixed costs	200	100
Operating profit	100	100

In the base case, in Table 1.1, both companies have sales of 1,000 but Company A has higher operational gearing, with higher fixed costs and lower variable costs than Company B.

When sales are reduced by 30 per cent we see, from Table 1.2, that Company B, with lower operational gearing, performs better.

Table 1.2

	Company A	Company B
Sales	700	700
Variable costs	490	560
Fixed costs	200	100
Operating profit	10	40

On the other hand, when sales increase by 30 per cent we see, in Table 1.3, that the benefit is reversed and Company A, with its higher operational gearing, performs better. An identical effect results from financial gearing.

Table 1.3

	Company A	Company B
Sales	1,300	1,300
Variable costs	910	1,040
Fixed costs	200	100
Operating profit	190	160

Bear in mind that costs that are fixed in the short term may not be fixed over a longer period. Some labour costs may, for example, be impossible to shed over a three-month period, perhaps because of contractual compensation, but are variable from the perspective of six months.

Earnings per share (EPS)

These calculations can be useful, particularly if a business issues new shares to raise money, to acquire other businesses or to reward staff. The calculation is to divide profits after tax by the number of shares that are issued. It is usual to assume that all share options are taken up and other convertible instruments are converted (adjusting the profitability for interest on the cash raised). This is referred to as the 'fully diluted EPS'. Another common measure of performance is earnings before interest tax, depreciation and amortisation (EBITDA). This looks at the underlying performance of the business, discounting the effects of more or less borrowing, changes in tax circumstances and depreciation policies.

All these measures are industry- or company-specific. They are useful business tools so tailor them to your needs and circumstances. A software house, for example, may have sky-high margins because so much of its cost base is devoted to product development, and it might be wise to include a proportion of those development costs in stocks and the cost of sales.

Keep it truthful

If this business plan is going to be handed to a financier or an investor or a bank then you do not want to be giving an incorrect view. Really, you don't. The most obvious temptation to mislead is where there has been a bad year that you feel was not representative and you may be tempted to adjust to correct what you feel is a misleading impression. Don't. There is a high risk of being found out together with a risk of incurring a legal liability and, once you earn a bad reputation, you will never correct it. Deal with facts you feel give an unfair impression by explaining them in words and, by all means, show – in addition to the historic figures – a pro forma set that shows well-explained adjustments.

The other temptation is to give the best possible interpretation of the future, which is the right thing to do, up to a point. Most people who go too far know full well when they have crossed the line. If the past shows pedestrian growth whilst the future figures show explosive growth, the reader will be sceptical. Even more important, don't fool yourself. The figures must be plausible.

Dealing with hard times

How is planning different when the market is tough or you in particular are suffering? Ask what has changed that ought to make a business plan today different from, say, a year ago. There are businesses that hold up well in a downturn and there are very few such periods where some businesses are not actually doing well. So ask, is that sales forecast still robust and are there reasons why you should be amongst the 20 per cent of good performers rather than the 80 per cent who are suffering? This leads on to the question of what can be done to move from the sufferers to the good performers category.

The second big area to look at is whether customers and suppliers are performing satisfactorily. Your plan should address the 'what ifs' such as what if a big customer or a major supplier failed, what contingency plans are there and what can be done to monitor the situation? For example, the collapse of the parent company of Entertainment UK, the UK's main music wholesaler, in the autumn of 2008 precipitated the collapse of Zavvi, one of the main music retailers, because it could not replace the source of supply and credit quickly enough.

The third big issue to consider is what opportunities are being thrown up when trading is tough. There may be opportunities to buy assets or businesses at bargain prices; or opportunities to change, driven by the accelerating changes in business practices and technology as people compete hard to improve their relative position.

Where is cost-cutting in your list? It should be there, but cost control should be in your organisational DNA anyway and will have been considered already so it should seldom be at the top of the list unless there is a problem of short-term survival. The quickest way to cut costs is usually to cut staff but this also closes off opportunities to expand or develop out of trouble.

Look at all these issues and amend your plan to take them into account. Re-run the numbers on the new assumptions and see what that tells you. You may have a nasty surprise, but whether or not it points to a crisis, once you have worked through them you have a firm picture of where you are that enables you to take a realistic look at strategy.

The business strategy in your business plan

Your strategy is central to your plan. Most of the time you just know what it is, but it does help to look at it formally with colleagues and review it and write it out. Without this formal review you may not really focus on ideas that aren't tenable any more and may not replace them with new and more appropriate ones. Don't worry about changing course; sticking with old ideas that aren't working is far worse than a bit of change.

Remember that a formal planning process seldom results in an effective and worthwhile business strategy. That is because the production of this plan focuses on processes rather than upon ideas. To get to the business plan you must analyse and get into detail, whereas a strategy is about ideas and, above all, about insights and a vision. So, to look again at your strategy you need to gather together a few people who really understand the markets you are in and how your business works, and have them throw around ideas that you can then discuss and work up into a strategy. If anyone tells you there is a formula for creating an effective strategy then they are fibbing: there is no magic formula for coming up with those penetrating insights. Google was created by two young, expert programmers who thought they could come up with a better idea for a search engine than Yahoo. The Prêt a Manger sandwich chain in London also emerged from two people throwing around ideas but, in their case, they set up one unit, ran it for a year and then decided that many of their ideas were wrong and what grew was very different from the original concept.

The linking factor behind all examples of successful strategies is that the drivers were not backroom people who were above the fray but people who were or became immersed in the detail of the operations. If there is a group who are set to review or create a business strategy then make sure it involves people who really know the 'sharp end', who know about the operations and the customers.

The numbers matter, of course – I am an accountant myself – but get the order right: the ideas come first and lead to the numbers. In these examples the creators of Google and Prêt a Manger originated some great ideas and then looked at making money from them. Even today, Google pursues some marvellous ideas where it is not obvious how they will earn money. Maybe the next edition of this book will admit that some of them never generated a profit, but the point still holds. And, since a high proportion of creative and entrepreneurial ideas don't work, the more that are tested and tried the more likely any business is to hit upon success.

The productivity boundary

One approach to strategy is to devote your business to improving its processes and performance. This sounds like a good idea but it contains the kernel of a problem: your competitors are all trying to do the same thing. What is more, if you improve your processes and reduce your costs so you steal a march on your competitors they will try to copy your ideas: they can hire some of your staff; they can see what you are doing by buying your products or talking to your customers and distributors. Your advantage is therefore temporary. Of course it is worth having the advantage, even for a relatively short time, but eventually both you and your competitors will hit the productivity boundary where you are as efficient as you can get. Long before then you will find that the benefits of all the hard work of improvement actually ends up in the pockets of your customers and your distributors as you reduce prices to match your competitors who are themselves improving their processes and cutting costs to undercut you and win over your customers.

Sustainable strategy

So what you are looking for is a sustainable strategy, one that confers a long-term advantage that is hard to copy. I believe all detailed strategies will fit into only three categories: monopoly, barriers to entry and being different. There can be some blurring between these categories, such as sheer size and dominance of a market – is that a monopoly or a barrier to entry? It may enable a

business to achieve economies of scale that would require any
potential competitor to endure years of losses to replicate.

Monopoly

The best strategy must be to have a monopoly of some sort. If
you have the best location in town then you have a monopoly and
can charge higher prices. If you are located on top of the only coal
or salt mine or source of clay for bricks then you have an
unassailable advantage. If you are a casino with a government
licence then you are a monopolist. If you have a large bookshop
or any other shop in a town that really won't sustain more selling
space devoted to that product then you have a monopoly – not
quite such a complete one because someone can come in with a
loss-leader, determined to drive you out of business, or they
might just make a mistake. For example, our bookshop business
was suddenly confronted by a large edge-of-town competitor that
was forced to close eventually because it was excessive for that
location, but not before it had forced us to close our shop too. So
the types of monopoly include:

- **location;**
- **regulation;**
- **contractual, such as being sole distributor of a product;**
- **patent or secret know-how;**
- **size and dominance.**

Barriers to entry

If you have high barriers to entry into your markets then you
are hard to beat and your strategy will focus on reinforcing those
barriers and building them higher. Having patents on your
technology both gives you a sort of monopoly and also creates
barriers to entry because competitors, even if they can do it, may
have to spend more than you to mimic the effects you can
achieve.

Having a strong brand also creates a barrier to entry. Coca-
Cola and Levi Jeans have maintained massive benefits over
decades through defence of their brands. It would cost a fortune

to displace them, but brands can still be overthrown; remember that vacuum cleaners are still referred to as 'Hoovers' despite the fact that Dyson has been the market leader for years.

Aircraft builders and engine manufacturers have fabulous barriers to entry. It would cost a new competitor an enormous amount to build the factories, to develop the know-how, to get clearances and approvals from governments and regulators, or to achieve the brand recognition. It would scarcely be worth it unless the government of a large country wanted to underwrite the costs for the purpose of building national prestige.

Being different

If you engage in different activities or do the same activities differently from your competitors then you can build a strong and sustainable strategy. All of the things you do will reinforce your difference and will make your strategy hard to copy. A good example might be low-cost airlines; these cannot be easily copied by the full-price airlines because there are so many reinforcing differences: they cut costs by not providing services (except at a price), by flying to out-of-town airports, by using only standard equipment, by putting rows of seats closer together, by limiting baggage allowances, and by having few people handling complaints. These are hard for the full-service airlines to replicate individually; they cannot easily move their seats around in the cabin, they cannot remove and put back cooking facilities, they already fly to major airports, they already have higher overheads to support their activities and they use different equipment for different routes.

Each time you make a choice about what activity your business will engage in or how it will do it you are also excluding other options, so there are trade-offs. In the example above, deciding to be a low-cost airline precludes the organisation from offering full-service routes and vice versa.

The management of the McDonald's fast food empire allowed virtually anyone to visit its restaurants and see behind the scenes. It sees its uniqueness as coming from dozens of individual factors that all reinforce each other and contribute in aggregate to that difference. The evidence is that, whether you like the product or not, there are hundreds of other fast food chains in the world but none quite like McDonald's; whether it is the menu or the taste or the ambience, the experience is different. McDonald's would probably argue that the way it manages its staff and the whole company culture is part of that unique way of doing things that confers a competitive advantage and is hard to copy.

Although this is a powerful approach it is important to adopt it with a self-critical spirit. There are many organisations that proclaim they are different and have a unique spirit and ethos when that is simply untrue. A good example is the Mecca Leisure Group which, in the 1980s, bought Pleasurama, an even bigger leisure company. Mecca had a very strong identity and corporate culture which, it would argue, drove it to outperform competitors. Fact or fantasy, I believe the culture could not survive the acquisition of a much bigger company. Suddenly there were divisions of people who were disgruntled and unhappy with the new management, and the annual company-wide party that had been such a morale booster in previous years was seen as a vast waste of money by the newly acquired staff. A culture that had worked with a fairly downmarket product range was less appropriate to upmarket casinos and hotels where staff were rather disdainful about the razzamatazz and showmanship; and what worked in one country did not work so effectively across several. The combined company continued to proclaim its difference and its corporate culture long after it became clear that there were actually two antagonistic cultures.

There is another long-term strategic technique that I came across recently in a newspaper, which was called 'last man standing'. It is really a non-strategy and seems a high-risk approach but could work in deteriorating markets where, one by one, the players go out of business until there is only one left. Presumably the final competitor in the market would make monopoly profits for a while as the market continued its decline. Meanwhile regulators would have little scope to find any one else to provide competition.

Risks, contingencies and scenarios

Risks change when the economic times are tougher. It is far easier to be optimistic when sales go up each year and the only issue is ensuring that they rise faster than costs. When sales and costs fall, so may the prices you obtain for your products and services. The problem this poses is that potential customers hold off buying because they hope that prices will drop further before they have to buy.

In bad times there is a temptation to believe that things have got as bad as they can and will now head upwards. This is illustrated by the rather gory term from the financial world – a 'dead cat bounce'. This states that even a dead cat will bounce back up a bit if it drops from a great enough height. It is true that there are forces within economic systems that mean that economies do recover: the simplest of these is the de-stocking cycle. Companies in aggregate do reduce their stocks of finished goods in a downturn in order to release cash and, eventually, they are forced to rebuild those stocks in order to stay in business and that, in turn, increases the business of those who supply them. The problem for someone writing a business plan is twofold: first, markets tend to overshoot both on the way up and on the way down; secondly, you have no idea where you are in the cycle. If you knew exactly when the 'turning point' arrived you would soon be very rich. Therefore, there is always still 'downside' risk however bad you think things are. Entrepreneurs will usually underestimate the risk of things getting worse whilst financiers may (now) overestimate it.

Break-even

Break-even is the point at which your profit is zero: more sales and you make a profit, less and you make a loss. It is a rough rule of thumb that helps to give you a sense of how vulnerable the business is and how easily you can survive in the face of a short-term problem, but don't read too much into it.

No bank will want to provide finance for a business that is only breaking even. If a 10 per cent fall in sales reduces you to break-even then you are very high risk; if it takes 50 per cent then pretty low risk. Cash is what matters to a business so the point of zero profit is still not adequate to survive in the long term because cash will be needed for capital expenditure and to invest in stocks and, if there is an upturn in fortunes, in debtors.

How should you calculate your break-even level of sales? It should not just be a matter of reducing the sales figure in your forecasts: you should also adjust the costs that you could clearly cut. In the very short term this would include cost of sales but not labour costs unless you can make workers redundant or reduce their numbers by natural wastage quickly. It is reasonable to show a reduction in costs that could be achieved within a month or so but, for example, if you cannot cut property costs for a year or two, that is too long; you cannot include those.

To calculate what level of sales brings you to break-even you need to divide your costs into three categories; fixed, variable and semi-variable costs:

1. Fixed costs are those that don't vary with sales, like rent; you almost certainly can't cut this in the very short term.
2. Variable costs are inputs such as the materials you buy to manufacture whatever you sell or, if you are a software company for instance, the licence fees you pay that are directly related to the product you sell. As sales go up or down these costs change in proportion.
3. Semi-variable costs are those that will change a bit with sales levels but have an irreducible 'floor'. Labour costs are usually semi-variable; you can shed some staff but not all of them. Telephone charges and electricity are usually semi-variable because you will pay a monthly fixed charge plus a per-unit used rate.

Once you understand how these costs vary it should be fairly easy to calculate their change with sales and therefore what the break-even sales level is. You can use a spreadsheet analysis, a formula or just good old-fashioned trial and error. Don't try to be too exact because you will delude yourself into believing it really is possible to estimate these things to three decimal places – these are rough and ready estimates.

All this is helpful to you in managing your business and also if you are using the business plan to raise new money or even to persuade the bank to continue your existing facilities. Bank managers like to see that a business is robust and knowing what you would do if things went wrong must make the business seem more likely to ride out the bad times.

Skills planning

You must consider what skills you will need and make sure you explain in your business plan how you will recruit, develop and retain the right staff. People join and stay with companies not just because of the rate of pay but also because they see that the experience, including training, will advance their career. Staff development comes in many guises and does not have to mean spending money on training courses, though that may sometimes be appropriate. It is almost invariably cheaper to develop people's skills than to recruit anew. It's possible to over-promote someone you know but the risks are lower than with new hiring.

Start by considering business goals and strategies and identifying the skills you will need within the organisation to attain them. Whilst you may need to recruit for some skills it will generally be cheaper, less risky and better for morale to develop existing staff. Plan with your staff what skills you will need from them and that they may want to develop. A member of staff may want to develop skills that are not necessarily of direct or immediate relevance to your business but you may still feel it is worth supporting them in this. Often this development process may be part of an appraisal system, with targets being set and achievement measured and rewarded.

A significant part of skills development arises from giving

staff relevant experience at work. Supervisory skills, for example, will be developed by giving supervisory experience, perhaps in conjunction with some coaching from someone within the business. In turn, developing people's coaching skills has an immediate payback through enabling them to support other work colleagues and making them better managers.

If learning beyond what the organization can provide itself is required, there are many ways to facilitate this: allowing flexible working time or time off to study, or paying for staff to attend college or use distance learning. Larger organisations may have training provided in-house.

Scenarios

It is a good idea, while planning and examining risks, to consider disaster recovery planning. For example, a high proportion of businesses fail after a collapse of their computer systems. Do you have proper backups of your data, preferably off-site? Have you considered using internet-based backups or staff taking a backup off-site daily? It is clearly not practical to cover all eventualities but have you an idea of what to do if your electricity went out for a week, or the internet went down for a few days, or there was a fire or flood or a really severe flu outbreak? Are you properly insured for the eventualities that can be covered? Insurance can be expensive but it is wise to make sure that you have covered the big things that could go wrong.

Not strictly a business issue, but a religious group had planned for scenarios such as attacks on their premises. They decided that they would not try to protect empty buildings but would devote their resources to protecting their congregants. They set up a system whereby e-mails could be sent to all members, at the touch of a button, warning them not to go to the community's buildings. But someone asked, in a planning session, how the e-mails could be sent if the buildings were not to be approached. A good question, highlighting the fact that technology can provide good and relatively inexpensive solutions but you need planning sessions to tease out all the issues. Role-plays are useful, requiring people to say what they would do, action by action.

Recently published articles and books have focused on the fact that unlikely events are not as unlikely as we think. In the 1990s and the first decade of the 21st century financiers were planning financial instruments based on risk analysis that only looked back 10 or 20 years. They had forgotten that if you look back 50 or 60 years it becomes clear that some supposedly rare events are not as rare as all that. They had also forgotten 'systematic risk', which means that if there is an underlying cause for a bad thing to happen, it may also cause other bad things to happen, so they are not individual occurrences but linked events. A hypothetical example is that something makes the electricity grid crash, which brings down the internet, computers, heating, lighting, transport and telephones. Let us suppose that the grid comes up again within a half a day but there are all sorts of knock-on effects that take weeks to resolve. The telephone and internet are not fully back for several days, which means several days' lost sales and an inability to reorder stock, to keep accounts, issue invoices or do your banking. This may be an extreme example, but the internet is becoming as fundamental to many of our activities as the electricity supply and is vulnerable to deliberate attacks. The business plan should, in my opinion, refer to events such as loss of telephone connections (cables are frequently cut by accident) and the internet going down – it is not that unusual for individual service providers to have outages.

Other problems that are not so uncommon include bad weather, illness, strikes and economic downturn. It is not hard to plan what one would do if each of these were rather more severe than what we see as the 'norm', where we believe we can cope without special planning.

The linked nature of our business processes –not just computing – is easily illustrated by the likely effects of a prolonged strike at key fuel depots. Contingency plans would need to be put in place rapidly: the food distribution system tends to have only a few days' supplies in hand, increasing numbers of factories work on a 'just in time' basis, and key workers from nurses to railway staff would be unable to get to work. A serious, even if non-fatal outbreak of contagious illness would not only depress retail spending but also lead to a shortage of employees turning up for work.

Some scenarios will prove to have no solution but, in others, a little advance preparation will make all the difference.

2

Assessing projects

Buying assets or businesses, establishing a new venture and disposing of an existing business activity all represent projects that need to be assessed and evaluated. Let us assume that the project is of a size that justifies time and effort to analyse, which will depend upon its absolute size and its size relative to the whole business. Clearly a £2,000 investment will be material for a small business but represents 'small change' for a large one.

There is great debate about the different techniques for evaluating projects and many books on the subject yet the greatest problem is the most basic: getting a reasonable forecast of the outcome on which to apply these techniques.

My colleague was very keen to introduce digital 'listening posts' into our shops to replace existing analogue ones. The new units would allow customers to hear excerpts from a wide range of books on CDs that we sold and to place orders for ones not in stock, compared with the old units only playing a choice of three or four excerpts. An argument could be put forward that the presence of the units in our shops would have an impact on the whole ambience that would justify a relatively modest expenditure. Whilst thinking this was a nice idea in principle I looked at the costs and revenues involved and saw that, across our small chain, the introduction of the units would cost several thousand pounds a year at a time when we were short of money.

My colleague justified the expenditure with the argument that it would only take a couple of extra sales per week to offset the extra costs. This illustrates the problem: he wanted the units and therefore made a forecast to justify them. I argued that the extra sales were speculative, represented a significant percentage increase in the then current sales levels and probably would not occur. Detailed costing showed we would need more extra sales than were forecast to offset the additional costs. I also argued that the existing units we had in place were probably a waste of money and that the true cost to be analysed was not the additional cost but the total cost, assuming that our alternative was not to retain the old units but to remove them and stop paying rent on them.

After a lot of bad feeling we compromised by putting in a couple of test units in one shop. For the curious, I was right: the units were scarcely used, led to no extra sales and did not justify the extra cost. Whether being right was worth the bad feeling is another matter.

This example illustrates several important points:

1. People often make forecasts to justify what they want to do rather than distancing themselves and making a dispassionate estimate.
2. Emotional attachment to or against a project can cause significant problems within a business.
3. Choosing the correct 'alternative' to a project is very important and affects the whole case.

In this illustration the use of best case/worst case scenarios or sensitivity analysis would not help but in other circumstances these are helpful techniques.

Another important issue to be addressed, which is not brought out above, is the length of time to be considered and what happens at the end of that time. In the example, I thought just one year's figures showed the project was not viable, so I went no further. Suppose the figures showed positive cash flows after the first year and that the equipment would have to be replaced after five years; then it is appropriate to evaluate the project over five years. In some cases a project or equipment may have a residual value at the end of the period and it may be important to try to estimate that value because it can affect the whole evaluation process.

Having established a forecast to evaluate, the next step is to turn it into a projected cash forecast. It is cash flows that matter to a business and not accounting rules, so it is cash that must be evaluated.

Discounted cash flow

There are several techniques for evaluation that all use principles of discounted cash flow. This is based on the simple premise that £1,000 today must be worth £1,100 next year if I can invest the money at 10 per cent interest for a year. Conversely, if I expect to receive £1,000 in 12 months' time that is equivalent today to:

£1,000 / (1+10%), which is £909.09.

And, £1,000 12 months after that is today worth:

£1,000 / (1+10%) x (1+10%), which is £826.45.

If we take all the future forecast cash flows and discount each back to today's value and add them up, the result is called the 'net present value' and, as long as that is a positive number then the project is profitable. If there was no initial cost then the two cash flows of £1,000 over two years would be worth £1,735.54 at the outset.

Another approach is to see what discount rate would bring the net present value to zero; that rate of return is called the 'internal rate of return' for the project.

All of this is straightforward except that the second big question, after having agreed a set of cash flows to discount, is what discount rate to use? The full answer is technically complex and based upon analysis of what rates of return are expected for similar projects by quoted companies. For smaller companies it is common to ignore the theory and set a 'hurdle' rate of return that is higher than the returns expected by investors in your company. Theorists explain that the particular riskiness of your project should not affect the rate set because an investor can always spread the risk by investing in other projects. However, in practice, one cannot make assumptions about the investment behaviour of your investors and it is usual to set a higher return for what is perceived as a more risky project.

There are problems with taking this approach that sets a high but fairly arbitrary desired rate of return. It could rule out a very low risk project that may show a modest return but still significantly better than the 'risk-free' return of putting money in government bonds and earning interest. It is also susceptible to someone intentionally setting an unfairly high (or low) discount rate to distort the result. The best way to deal with this is to have an agreed target level of return for projects in different business areas where the risk is related to the type of industry. It goes wrong when different returns are set for different categories of project and can be distorted by office politics.

I worked for a large leisure company that set a low target rate of return for what it termed 'maintenance investment', which was money spent to preserve existing income streams, and a higher rate for completely new projects. The failings of this scheme are set out below but they were accentuated in this case because, bizarrely, a company in old fashioned, shrinking markets had acquired another business in growing markets within the broad field of leisure activities. This meant that as members of the 'winning team', the managers of the failing markets captured an unfair proportion of available investment to prop up their businesses whilst the businesses with better prospects were starved of investment.

The fallacies of the approach are twofold. First, if the base business is making a poor return then whatever the forecasts say, it stands to reason that money invested in that business will, on average, earn the poor return of the overall business area. Without going into the accounting and forecasting sleight of hand, trust me, that is inevitably what happens. Secondly, the correct comparison is not to say, 'If we don't invest then profits in this business area will collapse.' The correct approach is to say, 'This is a declining business, let us not pour good money after bad but think of a way to dispose of the business or run it down to get as much cash as possible out of it.'

If a project can be seen as quite separate from the business area within which it sits then evaluate it on a standalone basis. However, in the case of this profit maintenance investment the project is inextricably bound up with the business area. The correct approach is to evaluate the project's cash flows together with those of the business area. The difficulty is in identifying and valuing the alternative 'base case'. However, if one believes the business could be sold for, say, £5 million, that sum you forego is the opportunity cost of further investment; add the project investment and then evaluate the cash flow from the continuing business including the project.

The leisure company's highly rated management team failed to understand that different discount rates apply to industry types and their inherent volatility, and not to the perceived risk of different categories of investment. In fact the total risk of 'maintenance investment', including the market volatility element, the forecasting risk and other risk specific to the project, was greater than for completely new projects.

Use of internal rates of return gets away, partly, from the problem of deciding an appropriate discount rate. If there are a series of potential projects that seem to have very high rates of return then, simply, they are preferred to those showing lesser rates of return and if capital for investment has to be rationed then they will be the ones chosen. The problem of an appropriate discount rate is still there for borderline projects.

In the past businesses have used measures of an appropriate discount rate such as 'weighted average cost of capital' (WACC).

This appears, superficially, to be simpler and more related to specific business needs, but that is an illusion. To calculate it you would need to know what rate of return equity investors are expecting as well as what interest rates are paid on borrowing and then, using a weighted average of them, you find a discount rate. It implies that two identical businesses that just happen to have a different proportion of debt to equity and therefore different WACC would therefore value an identical project differently, which makes no sense.

Other evaluation methods

The old-fashioned evaluation methods are often adequate for smaller businesses, suffering the same problem as any method that potential forecasting errors swamp any other consideration but they have the benefit of relative simplicity.

Payback

The simplest technique is to see how quickly a project pays back its investment, but it appears to suffer the crucial flaw that it looks no further forward than the point when repayment is achieved. Clearly if the returns fell to zero at that point then few people would judge the project a success, albeit the business had not lost money. In practice the technique calls for a little flexibility and common sense. If there is a payback of, say, two years then for most investors that would seem quick and a very high return and one would assume the fast generation of cash would continue. If the forecaster knows that cash generation will actually fall away quickly after two years then they need to say so, at the same time as publishing the rapid payback.

To illustrate the disadvantage, consider an investment of £1,000 into either project A or project B, with the cash flows shown in Table 2.1.

Table 2.1

Year	Project A	Project B
0	−1,000	−1,000
1	200	50
2	400	150
3	600	250
4	200	350
5	100	400
6	100	400

Both projects return £1,600 over six years on a £1,000 investment but project A has a much faster payback of two years and four months compared with four years and six months for B. If both projects cease after six years then clearly A, with its faster return, is preferable. However, if Project A continues generating £100 per annum for four years whilst B continues at £400 per annum, then it is not so clear. Actually an internal rate of return calculation would show A has a 21.9 per cent return whilst B has 22.2 per cent, making it marginally preferable. However, all other things being equal, you might still select Project A rather than Project B if you feel there is greater forecasting risk over the longer term when B wins its advantage.

Accounting rate of return

The accounting rate of return (ARR) is calculated by taking the profit and loss effect of the proposed investment and dividing this by the amount invested. It has the benefit of simplicity and the serious flaw of ... simplicity. The ARR gives answers in the same terms that are reported to investors and is immediately understandable, but it takes no account of the time value of money and so a profit recorded in five years' time is accorded the same weight as one recorded tomorrow. It has no way of distinguishing between an investment made tomorrow and the further monies that will need to be put into the project next year.

The problems are illustrated in Table 2.2. There is a potential five-year project that requires investment of £2,500 over the period and will produce total profits of £3,900 over the period. For simplicity we will assume that profit and cash flow from trading are identical so that the total cash flow of investment and trading is shown on the bottom line of the table.

Table 2.2

Year	0	1	2	3	4	5
Investment	−1,000	−750	−750			
Profit		200	400	400	1,400	1,500
Cash flow	−1,000	−500	−500	400	1,300	1,500

The project returns £3,900 over the period on an investment of £2,500, which is an ARR of 30 per cent, which sounds quite attractive. However, the big returns occur at the end of the project, in years four and five, so the internal rate of return is only 15 per cent, which is much less attractive. This shows that whilst the ARR is simple and easily understood it can also give incorrect answers for projects with complex cash flows and for those with higher returns further in the future.

Postscript

After pursuing projects that have been approved it is important to look back at the results in order to improve future decision making. It must be acknowledged that such a review is subject to all the same possible flaws as the original decision but it should still be done in the hope that lessons may be learnt. Such a review will become academic if left too long so, except in the case of very large projects, it is usually best to conduct it 12 months after the project commences.

Pursuing the example given above of the leisure company

that allocated a lower rate of return threshold for projects defined as 'low risk' maintenance of profits, it too had a system of reviewing investment outcomes. However, since the original methodology was wrong in ignoring the declining core business, so was the review. It can be difficult to separate project cash flows from the business within which it resides. Where separation proves impossible it is, therefore, important to look back at the whole business area that includes the project. In the example, such a review would have highlighted serious problems but, by allowing the business areas to focus just on capital investment projects, they were able to manipulate the results to show they had been successful.

In the example, many people were guilty but ultimate responsibility for the system and its wilful blindness always lies at the top of the organisation. Within just a couple of years this approach led to the collapse of a very large company. No book, no theoretical system, no rules will ensure wise decisions. The key to good decision making, as with good governance, is not to build a complex edifice of rules that people will use great ingenuity to subvert but to employ integrity in the first place.

Business acquisitions

A business acquisition is simply a particular version of an investment project and all the same issues discussed previously apply. However, the word 'simply' may be misplaced because there is often far more complexity.

It can be harder to forecast future cash flows and so acquirers may use expected strategic advantages to reach decisions. Suppose you believe that by acquiring business B and applying skills from your current business A then you will not only be able to increase cash flows but also open new areas of opportunity that you find hard to forecast. You can try to make those forecasts and evaluate the cash flows, or you may use 'soft logic', analyse the strategic benefits and make a decision without recourse to numbers.

There may be logic to forecasting the combined accounts of the merged business because short-term pressures may outweigh any long-term cash flow benefits. After all, if attractive long-term benefits come at the expense of a negative short-term impact on earnings or greater borrowing requirements or a reduction in balance sheet values, then it is useless to ignore the practical difficulties they may create. Theory suggests that profitable projects will always be financed because markets are efficient: theory is wrong. So there may be cases where the economic case for making an acquisition could be overwhelmed by short-term problems or even just by accounting ones.

Because of the difficulty of forecasting future cash flows, particularly as the target business becomes bigger, it is common for companies to forecast the effect of combining the two businesses, particularly on earnings per share (EPS). The way this is done is in two stages; first to take the most recent possible forecast or actual balance sheet of both businesses, then to combine them whilst taking account of any payment to shareholders, changes in shareholdings, reduction or increase in borrowings, fees and other costs associated with the acquisition and any anticipated effect of a fair value exercise. Similarly, the profit and loss accounts of the two businesses are added together, with all the relevant adjustments, expected reduction in costs or increases in profitability. A reconciling funds flow statement connects the balance sheet and P&L. These sets of accounts are called 'pro forma' to highlight the way they have been produced and that they are not detailed forecasts but a 'best guess'. When reading pro forma accounts it is very important to read and consider the assumptions that have been used to draw them up.

From these pro forma accounts it is possible to calculate the earnings per share of the combined entity and, hopefully, demonstrate that the acquisition will have a beneficial effect. EPS is calculated by taking profit after interest and tax and dividing by the number of shares in the acquiring company (after the deal), as adjusted for any share options or similar instruments it may have. To all intents and purposes this EPS calculation acts as a proxy for a net present value calculation simply because that would be so difficult to do even if one had full access to the accounting records of the business being acquired.

Goodwill

If a business you acquire has an accounting net worth of £1,000 whilst you pay £1,500 for it, the difference of £500 is called 'goodwill'. However, there are adjustments to be made before making this calculation. First, you would adjust the target's assets for any differences in accounting policies; then you would examine the acquired assets and apply 'fair values' to them before making this calculation. This process will include revaluing properties and considering the real value to the business of the assets. An example of the effect this can have would be the acquisition of a business that has computers or tills in use that have been depreciated to zero value. Clearly, if they are in use, they do not have zero value to the business and should be revalued to an appropriate figure. Overall the result can be either an increase or decrease in balance sheet value. That means it is possible to have negative goodwill, which occurs when you pay £1,500 for the business but find the revalued assets are worth £2,000.

Unfortunately, great ingenuity has been devoted by acquiring companies to ensure that the 'fair value' exercise results in a diminution in the value of assets acquired and the setting up of as many provisions in the accounts as possible. A provision is simply a charge against the P&L account that can be released against an expense anticipated to occur at a later date. It is therefore simply a change in timing and also in labelling. The sleight of hand occurs when the provision is associated with the acquisition and becomes part of the goodwill that is written off but is viewed as being outside normal trading. When it turns out to be unnecessary and is written back, or if it is released against expenses that may or may not be strictly related to the acquisition, then lo and behold it comes back as part of 'normal' trading and can give the impression of a business trading better than it really is. Writing down the value of fixed assets reduces future depreciation charges and writing down the value of stocks increases future trading income. Sometimes these provisions and adjustments are perfectly legitimate, but at other times they are designed to give readers of accounts, be they investors or lending banks, a misleading view of the business. Many of the potential abuses have been stopped by changes in accounting standards but some can still be slipped through.

How goodwill is treated in the accounts of a company will depend upon the accounting standards followed. EU listed companies follow International Financial Reporting Standards (IFRS) that differ in this respect from previous UK Financial Reporting Standards (FRS). Whereas the latter allow goodwill to be kept on the acquiring company's balance sheet and amortised over up to 20 years, the former prohibit amortisation. Both require an annual review of goodwill to ascertain whether its value has been impaired during the year. There is yet another set of standards followed by small companies in the UK. This is a complex area and rules change frequently, so any company that is making an acquisition and produces accounts will need to consult its accountants to check what rules apply.

3

The budget process

What is a budget and why does a business need one?

A budget is just a business plan that covers a defined period and describes, in numbers, the activity of a business. It mimics the financial accounts, recording the expected income and costs for a profit and loss account, the cash movements for a cash flow and the end-of-period balance sheet. Unlike the financial accounts of the business it looks forwards, usually for one year, instead of backwards.

Its purpose is twofold: 1) to forecast where the business is going and what the implications are, such as a need for extra machinery, and to decide on necessary actions if the predicted outcomes are unacceptable; 2) to act as a business discipline during the year, allowing regular reviews of progress against budget so you can analyse why things are different from expectations and decide on what to do to correct adverse variances or reinforce favourable ones.

The purpose of a budget is not to go through a repetitive,

unthinking ritual: the purpose is to help the analysis of what is going on and to lead to actions. The budget is like a navigation chart for a ship. You know where you are trying to get to and you plot a course (the budget) and as you move along and veer away from the planned course, you use the chart to guide you to take actions to get back on course so that you can get to your destination or, if you will miss it, decide whether that causes you a big problem and, if it does, what to do.

There are different types of budget. The basic one starts with a level of sales activity and works out the associated costs. However, some enterprises use 'activity based budgeting' or 'flexible budgeting' where a formula is used to calculate budget costs from business activity and the reported budget, each month, will depend upon the level of business activity. This is pretty complicated and I will focus on the more traditional budget.

Explicit assumptions

There's an old joke about *assume* making an *ass* of *u* and *me*. We assume things and don't really examine those assumptions and don't appreciate that they may be wrong and what the consequences would be.

Make your assumptions for the budget explicit. Write them down: 5 per cent increase in sales, 3 per cent increase in business property taxes, no increase in rent, 3 per cent wage rise in January, no increase in staff numbers, no training budget, etc. Make clear the zero changes because these can be very significant. You choose, for example, not to have a training budget, which is easy to do but it may represent an important business decision that you should consider in depth, not just skate over.

Discuss these assumptions with your colleagues before they get cast in stone. Make sure they not only agree with your forecasts but also buy in to the decisions they imply. If your operations manager thinks that cutting out training is a very bad idea and possibly unsustainable, then don't just make the assumption, work through a budget and present the end result as a fait accompli. Remember that budgets can also force decisions. When the operations manager comes back after six months and says that three people really need to go on a health and safety course and you respond, 'Sorry, there is no budget', that leads to friction and possibly adverse real-world consequences if the business fails an inspection due to a lack of essential training.

A budget is very much a joint enterprise. It is absolutely not something that should be produced by the finance function in isolation and then presented to the people who have to make it happen. Involving the people who have to work within the budget during the early stages of putting it together helps them become committed to it. If they are involved only episodically, perhaps to sketch out some assumptions and to review the end result, the danger is that they do not use the budget to guide their decisions and are not committed to making it happen.

Start with sales

The place to start is not with what costs were last year but with what you expect sales to be in the forthcoming year. Most businesses will want to produce a detailed monthly budget covering the forthcoming year, often with a less detailed forecast covering another year or two. The forecast level of sales in any month is likely to be based upon what was achieved in the previous year, adjusted for underlying changes in demand, in pricing and maybe for details such as the number of trading days in the period. Clearly that means you do not want to set the budget too far in advance of the year-end because you will be missing some months of data. However, you should not just use last year's figures without thought. Ask yourself what is happening in the business, what is changing. If everything were just staying the same, after all, you would not need to bother with a budget.

So, start with the current year's actual figures and forecast for the balance of the year. Don't just use the budget for the months remaining of the current year unless you are confident that is the best forecast. Then review the broad changes that are taking place. It is really useful to look back at previous years' outcomes to remind yourself of trends. If sales show a trend decline and you are showing an upturn, what is it you have planned that you see as bringing about this change?

Work up the sales in detail; don't just add a percentage to this year's figures. You are going to produce a cash budget as well as one for the P&L, so timing does matter. If significant costs or sales fall into one month or the other, that can affect whether you can pay your bills at the month end.

Work up the costs

So you have the sales budget by month or by week or even by day. Work from this to derive the cost element of the budget. The sales forecast defines when stocks must be in-hand and when they will be paid for, and similarly for some bought-in services such as transport. To the extent that costs such as labour and utilities can vary to some extent with output (remember that even if you do not adjust staff numbers by month you may still utilise more or less overtime) calculate these and put them into the budget.

The costs should always be checked to make sure that each category represents the same percentage of sales as in previous years. If they don't, then don't force the numbers to conform: it is important to understand why they are different.

The balance sheet and cash flow

As well as producing a budget profit and loss account for each year, you will want to produce a cash budget and a balance sheet.

You need the cash budget to make sure that you have enough cash to run the business and, if a deficit is shown, to reveal if you need to adjust the timing of your spending, raise money from a bank or go to shareholders.

The cash flow differs from the profit and loss account in two ways; the timing of events is different, and there are some items that appear in one but not in the other.

Timing

The profit and loss account recognises sales income when you sell the product but the cash flow recognises it when you receive payment. Similarly the P&L recognises costs that are associated with the sale when that occurs but the cash flow recognises costs when the money is paid out.

The differences in timing can be significant in the case of a tax charge shown in the P&L but not actually paid for years.

Items in one but not the other

The cash flow will include capital expenditure but the P&L will only recognise the element of capital expenditure that is included in the annual depreciation charge. The cash flow will not show the depreciation charge at all because it is not a cash item.

Imagine a company spends £10,000 plus sales tax of £1,750 on a new item of equipment at the beginning of its financial year, which is expected to have an economic life of 10 years. It is depreciated over 10 years on a straight-line basis (in this case), which means a depreciation charge of £1,000 per year or £83.33 per month.

We will assume that the sales tax is Value Added Tax as applies in the UK and that the business is registered for VAT. So the £1,750 is not shown as a cost of the machinery in any accounts; it does not appear at all in the P&L. Rather, it appears in the cash flow as 'cash out' when it is paid and as 'cash in' when it is repaid by HMRC. The balance to this is that it is shown in the balance sheet as a debtor when it is paid and disappears when it is repaid.

The cash flow shows the £10,000 paid for the machine when it is paid. The balance sheet shows the £10,000 as a fixed asset when the machine is installed and shows the same sum as a creditor until it is paid for, at which point the creditor disappears and bank cash is reduced by £10,000. The depreciation charge is shown in the P&L, increasing at £83.33 per month.

Another item that will not appear on the P&L is expenditure on stocks, as raw materials, as work in progress or as finished goods waiting to be sold. Until they are sold these stocks are not relevant to the P&L. The costs this applies to will include not just the cost of bought-in items but labour directly attributable to these stocks and also a proportion of the overheads attributable.

The balance sheet will show what your financial ratios look like but will also allow you to check your calculations, because the budgeted P&L, cash flow and balance sheet must all reconcile.

Budget commentary

As with producing monthly accounts, the commentary that accompanies the budget does not only provide an explanation to the reader; it also helps to check that the figures are correct. As one goes through explaining why sales are up or down and why the margins are up or down, why property costs have risen and how overheads have been reduced, mistakes become obvious and can be corrected.

The order in which the commentary is dealt with should follow that of the accounts, starting with the P&L, going through sales, margin, staff costs, property costs, overheads, depreciation, financial costs and taxation; then the balance sheet and the funds flow that links the starting and closing balance sheet and the P&L. If there are material non-cash items in the funds flow then a separate cash flow is needed and an explanation of that too.

Reviewing the budget

It is the budget review that really matters. A budget should always be reviewed by someone who did not have a hand in preparing it so that there is an independent eye looking at it.

Unfortunately many businesses take the expected outcome for the current year, add 5 per cent to everything and set it as the budget for next year. That is easy but is it helpful? We make choices and decisions in business and it is these that the budget should shine a light on. So the budget review should not just check the arithmetic – though that must be done – but look at and question the assumptions, the choices and the actions that lie behind the budget. Every budget should always have a section detailing the important assumptions that lie behind the figures:

- **What changes in the business are assumed in the budget?**
- **What changes in the environment are assumed?**
- **Will the same staffing levels be maintained?**
- **Are improved efficiencies possible?**
- **Is there sufficient provision for training, marketing or R&D?**

The review should also compare trends over three or four years for the key numbers and ratios, particularly sales, gross margin and labour costs as a percentage of sales. The gross margin is particularly important because a small over-optimistic difference here can have a big distorting effect, as illustrated in the example below.

Most financial managers will try to have some hidden fat in the budget so that if things turn out less favourably than expected they will have something to balance it out. I tend to think one should not force out every bit of this in the review – it is fair enough to leave some flexibility as long as there is not so much hidden that it affects business choices.

Wishful thinking

The big problem with budgeting is the human response. Have we all been there, writing a budget that describes where we want to be but really, deep in our hearts, we don't believe will happen? There are two causes of this: outside pressure or self-delusion.

I have been through budgeting processes where the group managing director has received the budget from a division and told them that it is unacceptable. So they go away and come back with another budget that has the required profit outcome. In theory this is a reasonable process but, in practice, there is a severe risk that the divisional managers have simply adjusted their forecasts to be more optimistic.

An extreme example of this was a retail business where the gross profit was a calculated figure; it had to count its stocks at the year-end and value them using an assumed gross margin based upon the thousands of invoices for stock deliveries received during the year. To make it slightly more complicated, it was entirely possible for the mix of sales to be different from the mix of stocks in the business, so that the gross margin applied to what was sold could be slightly different from what was left in stock; nonetheless, having valued what was left in stock it was straightforward to calculate the gross profit of the sales achieved during the year. The group managing director was a forceful personality and, at the board meeting, took the divisional finance director through a back-of-envelope calculation to show that the gross profit had to be slightly higher than was shown in his initial budget; the original could not possibly be right. The managing director's amendment became the revised budget. Needless to say, it was wrong.

There is a simple equation to describe a business's cost of sales:

cost of sales = purchases + opening stock - closing stock

To achieve a higher gross profit means having a lower cost of sales. Since the purchases at the year-end are known from the accounting system and since the opening stock was calculated last year, the only thing that can be changed to achieve the target gross profit is the closing stock. As I said, for this business the stock value had to be calculated from an assumed gross margin. So, every year the stock value had to be assumed upwards ... and upwards ... and upwards. I think you can guess what happened eventually.

The lesson is straightforward. Budgets are very helpful tools for running businesses but require finance directors who can resist bullying and managing directors who can resist the temptation of short-term fixes that may come back to haunt them eventually.

The second issue, which I called 'self-delusion', is really more wishful thinking because you probably know that the budget is unlikely to be achieved. You make optimistic assumptions because the alternative is something you just don't want to think about and the actions you have to take if the worst case does turn up are unpalatable. I have been there myself: a business that grew during its early years but then sales began to fall. We could explain the fall and it was not totally unreasonable to imagine those causes had plateaued and modest growth might resume. In our case we took the appropriate actions for a worst-case outcome: we sought another, related business area to expand into. That does not detract from the fact that we put forward pretty optimistic budgets.

So how do you deal with outside pressures and your own wishful thinking? The only answer is to be aware of the issue. Optimistic budgets tend to have the effect of delaying difficult decisions and making the end-result worse. Look for new opportunities now. Make hard decisions now.

4

Cash

Cash is king, and being able to offer cash for products and services may win you a better price, not least because suppliers get paid immediately and there is no credit risk. Although they may also evade their taxes, if you have no particular reason to believe they are doing so then it is not your duty to enquire closely into their intentions, so don't be too shy about offering cash payment if a supplier will offer a lower price.

On a larger scale, having cash in hand will get you better deals when credit is tight. If a competitor falls into bankruptcy, having cash may enable you to buy the business cheaply or buy its assets or stocks cheaply.

Be aware of how much cash you have available. Take advantage of internet banking and make sure you know your bank balances each day. This does also mean that, if you trade on an overdraft, you know what that is too.

If you use internet banking you should take some security measures. The best precaution is to use a computer that does not have a web browser active, is not on a network and is not used for e-mails either. At the very least you must have good up-to-date anti-virus software and it is a good idea to use other anti-malware software too because no single package will neutralise all threats. There are lots of good freeware packages available over the internet that can be put on to a memory stick for transfer to the computer used for your banking. Ensure that only a small number of trusted people know the security passwords and make sure that there are authorisation limits. Be sure that more than one person looks at balances so that they act as a check on each other.

Manage cash

Think of your cash as a vital resource that needs careful managing. This means that you try to make sure that you extract cash from customers as quickly as possible and strictly control late payment. Whilst I believe strongly that businesses that are able to should pay their debts promptly because that is a moral way to trade, it also enhances your reputation and will stand you in good stead if trading is difficult for a short period. Nonetheless, if you are short of cash you must be aware of how to maximise your resource. You must also be aware of managing cash by thinking clearly about stock levels.

Debt recovery

Debt recovery works both ways: you may need to recover debts while you will want to know how to resist or delay similar action against you. After normal calls and letters asking for payment, the first formal step is usually to engage a debt recovery agency. Some accountancy firms operate these but there are plenty of others out there. For a fee that is usually based on the amount they recover, these agencies will chase the debtor, sometimes by letter, sometimes by telephone. Reputable agencies will usually be members of a trade association.

The debt recovery process

The debt recovery process starts with prevention, taking steps such as choosing your customers, monitoring them and managing them. It moves on to taking action to extract payment from reluctant debtors.

Choose your customers

It sounds obvious to say that a customer who does not pay is not worth having, but many businesses have people in sales and in accounts who have different mindsets. A sales-oriented person may often simply be focused on achieving sales and not on the reliability of being paid. Similarly, however good a customer may be, it is very easy to forget that if they delay paying for six months, even though you are certain they will pay eventually they can put immense pressure on the cash flow of your business. The effect is most severe with the best customers whose purchases are the largest.

Effective debt recovery starts with choosing your customers. This is easy to say and harder to do in practice because a business needs to sell in order to exist and if someone wants to buy and you need to sell .... Nonetheless it is striking how simple precautions are often not followed. When a customer starts dealing with you and you open an account for them, ask for and take up trade references. You would imagine that prospective customers will only give good references, but it is surprising how often they find it difficult to come up with anyone suitable, which should put you on your guard. I have been in the situation where this procedure has theoretically been in place but has not worked so I understand the difficulties. You are busy and each letter or telephone takes time, so you delay and then forget. Maybe you are embarrassed to start asking because you have left it too long; or someone lower down the organisation actually starts supplying the customer before references have been taken up; or the reference is not much use, they nominate a customer rather than a supplier or someone whose full address they don't give or someone who you can contact but who is not very forthcoming. You often feel unsure as a result of making enquiries.

What are you looking for from a reference? You want to know how long a customer has been trading because a long-established business is probably more secure than one just set up. You also want to know that they pay their debts and pay them on time. That is probably all you can find out. For larger businesses and larger transactions you should consider consulting credit rating agencies or looking at their accounts – you can ask for these if the transaction is substantial, or conduct a check through Companies House. A small company may take advantage of exemptions that mean that published accounts may not give much information; in that case you can ask for the detailed accounts that it will certainly have. A simple internet search may throw up another supplier's court action to recover debts or allow you to see their filed accounts, which would reveal late submission, heavy borrowings or a history of trading losses. You might do internet searches on the individual directors too. Be concerned if the proposed transaction is large in relation to their previous business. If the transaction is large, you may want to take out credit insurance. There are also credit agencies which, for a fee, will give a credit rating.

What are you looking for? Anything that makes you feel uncomfortable. What do you do with the results? That is more difficult. Consider carefully how much credit to give new customers initially; you can review this after you have established a trading history and built up confidence. You may want to monitor the account more closely, seek faster payment or you may not want to deal with them at all. Or you may take a view and ignore the results of your enquiries, perhaps because you know the directors and trust them, perhaps because the risk seems acceptable.

Monitor debtors

There is always a trade-off between the cost and benefit of monitoring your customers. Time devoted to this cannot be used on more productive things. However, most accounting systems will provide the minimum warnings of someone who is late in paying their bills or who exceeds their credit limit. These systems will also allow you to make notes so that you can look back at previous problems with each account. Businesses that give credit should always review their aged debtors lists each month and should devote priority to the larger debts and those most overdue.

Keep a note of when customers pay you late and keep an eye on regular customers who are delaying payment by increasing amounts. For example, if they pay three days late one month and a week late the next, it is already a sign for concern; if they pay 10 days late the next month then you may be well advised to reduce their credit limit – making sure your staff are aware of the change – and maybe you would want to telephone the customer to see if there is a specific problem you should know about. This process is as much about controlling your own staff as the customer because it is not unusual for people to accept orders from established customers without checking how much they owe. Ask yourself whether you are an important supplier to this customer, which may give you leverage in getting them to pay more promptly since you can slow down or limit deliveries to them.

In more difficult trading conditions it is common for your customers to try to stretch their credit with you. The problem you then have is that you may be left short of cash at the month-end to pay your own suppliers, and so it goes round. I believe you should always be tougher with your customers than your suppliers are with you – which leaves you better off in this spiral. Remember that if a customer is finding cash tight then you want them to squeeze another supplier, not you, so keep on their case and ensure that this is what happens.

Act and control

Most accounting systems will provide a facility to print and send monthly statements for overdue accounts. Do not ignore this: always send statements, as they remind those who have genuinely forgotten and send a message to those who are trying to delay that you have not forgotten. It also gives you a stick to beat those who claim they have lost the invoice: you can respond that you have been sending them statements.

If a customer is late in paying, always make a note on the system, detailing how much was paid and when, so that you can review it later. If the customer pays only part of what is due, perhaps raising a query on the rest, make a note of that too. Make sure your staff do all this and do not just ignore it. If a pattern of late payment emerges, talk to the customer's contact within your organisation and agree with them what to do – you do not want to upset a good customer but nor do you want to allow a serious credit risk to build up. If a customer learns that they can build up an overdue account of a few days or a few weeks then, if they have serious cash flow difficulties, it is you who will be used to plug that gap whilst their other supplier who chased promptly will be paid.

If your business is in the UK and your customers are individuals rather than companies then data you keep on them as individuals may fall under the Data Protection Act which may, in turn, require you to register with the Information Commissioner as a keeper of information. However, there is an exemption for processing data as part of keeping accounts and records (for accounting). So, as long as the data are factual and relate to legitimate accounting matters, such as dates and amounts of payment and queries raised, there should be no need to register.

If you have credit limits in place or you decide to apply sanctions, you must have systems in place so that everyone within your organisation who may be in a position to supply that customer is aware of the limit, how close the account is to that limit and what they must do. There is no point in having a credit limit if the alarm bells ring in the accounts department only some time after the organisation has supplied goods to a much greater value.

Manage problem accounts

There is an escalating range of actions you can apply to problems with customer accounts. You can start with a friendly conversation in which you ask them to observe credit terms, moving on to less friendly admonition, letters and threats, then reducing their credit limit, delaying supplies or withholding supplies completely.

In some countries it is possible or even an automatic right to charge interest on late payment of accounts, which provides a salutary warning. If you need a line in your terms and conditions or on each invoice to confer the right to charge interest then make sure it is there. In the UK the Late Payment of Commercial Debt (Interest) Act (1988) provides for interest at 8 per cent over the 'official dealing rate' as well as penalties to run from 30 days after delivery or invoice date (whichever is later). The right is automatically implied in UK contracts even if there is no notice of it on the body of the invoice. Even if you do not invoke the right it is useful to have the option and to be able to use the threat if necessary. At the same time, one must also be aware that some customers may react badly and take their business elsewhere. Others may challenge you to take them to court, which you may prefer not to do.

It should always be a rule that the range of possible sanctions in account management should be discussed and coordinated with whoever has sales responsibility for an account. This is because he or she knows the customer and should be able to make action more effective and avoid upsetting good customers. Not all late payers are a credit risk.

If you send threatening letters, perhaps with 'final demand' written across the top, then do make sure that it really is a final demand. If customers learn that they have weeks of letters to come that all say 'final demand', they are more likely to wait for the real one.

Letters can be firm but it is unnecessary and counterproductive to make them rude. After a period in the United States I remember receiving a demand for payment of a bill that started 'You have evaded this debt for too long ... '. I had no idea that there was any outstanding bill and was deeply offended by this approach and so, knowing there was no risk in the British courts, I ignored them. A more polite approach would have led me to look into the matter and see if I really did owe money.

Normally the final letter in this part of the process is one that threatens to refer matters to lawyers within a specified number of days – usually no more than a week.

Recovering debts

Once one gets beyond the range of reminders and chasers one is in the realms of extraction where stronger methods are required. However, these are more likely to cost money to implement so one must make sure not to pay fees to try to recover trivial debts or ones where you know the debtor can't pay.

Be careful not to use unlawful behaviour to recover debts nor to appoint an agency that may use unlawful behaviour: you could be liable for their actions.

Harassment

Harassment of people in debt by creditors or their agents is a criminal offence in the UK under the Administration of Justice Act 1970. It is unlawful in other countries too; if your business is based in another legal jurisdiction you will need to check the details of local laws. The issue, of course, is what constitutes 'harassment'. It is worthwhile for any UK business to be aware of the Office of Fair Trading Guidance on this. Whilst this code does not have the force of law it is likely to be persuasive in court proceedings. Its direct purpose is to guide what is appropriate behaviour by those individuals and bodies that need to be licensed under the Consumer Credit Act 1974 and breaches of it could lead to a loss of that licence. There are obvious behaviours that are banned, such as threats or violence, but falsely claiming authority or using documents that look misleadingly like official court documents are also banned.

Statutory demand

There is a powerful device available in the UK for obtaining payment, particularly from larger companies that can pay but will not do so and clearly owe a debt: issuing a winding-up petition. It is really only appropriate where you could contemplate a complete break in relations with the debtor. Even the threat of issuing a petition can be very powerful, and if it does not work then following up with a formal statutory demand can cost you nothing and frighten even the biggest companies. There is nothing to stop you issuing such a petition against even the very largest companies (as long as the debt is greater than the minimum of £750), when it is clear they can pay the debt if they are so minded. The reason why this is powerful is that it is extremely embarrassing. Complex loan agreements, for example, will usually have a default clause that refers not to a successful winding-up order but to the issue of a winding-up petition! The stages to go through are, first, to try all other methods of obtaining payment, then to threaten to apply for a winding-up order, then to issue a statutory demand that gives 21 days' notice of intention to issue a winding-up petition and, finally, to issue a petition to the court.

A statutory demand does not have to be issued through a court and may, therefore, cost you nothing. Clearly, however, it is psychologically more powerful if issued through a solicitor. Actually issuing a petition may be more fraught than threatening to do so. There is an immediate court fee of £150 and you will have to deposit some money as security for costs. The problem arises if the debtor is either bloody minded or can show they do not owe the money. Once you take the step of issuing a petition it is possible for them to tie you up in legal processes and demand you deposit monies with the court to cover the eventuality of your losing and having to pay costs. So, issuing a statutory demand is easy and risk-free but if you want to actually petition for a winding-up order then get legal advice – and also be confident the debtor can pay; there's no point spending money if they really are on the verge of bankruptcy.

The statutory demand must:

- **include details of the debtor and creditor, of the debt and consideration given for it;**
- **include the contact details of an individual at the creditor or their agent/solicitor who can discuss the matter;**
- **clearly state that it is a statutory demand and that it may lead to a winding-up petition after 21 days.**

If you are claiming for costs or interest, this amount must be included in the demand. There is a downloadable form 4.1 on the UK's Insolvency Service website. On this you will see that if your business receives a statutory demand that gives, for example, a call centre number and they will not put you through to the person noted on the document, the demand is invalid.

To provide the basis for a winding-up petition there would have to be evidence that the demand had been served, which can be done by post to the registered office or in person.

If you have received a statutory demand then consider whether you have a defence or a counterclaim. If you have, let the issuer know; they may choose to withdraw their notice. Remember that if they have not given you contact details of the signatory, including a telephone number, or if the phone number does not work, the statutory demand is invalid. Check that they have given you all the necessary information: if not, the document is invalid.

Dealing with bailiffs

Many countries have the equivalent of the bailiff, who has a role in seizing assets in the course of insolvency or to repay an outstanding debt. In France, for example, the title 'bailiff' is reserved for officers of the court who enforce court orders, whilst in the United States the bailiff has a wider role covering seizure but also being court security officers.

A bailiff is able to seize goods to sell at auction to satisfy an unpaid debt. The UK has different types of bailiff; some work for the courts whilst some are simply private firms working for businesses. They have different powers but can generally enter commercial premises, though usually not by force, and seize goods. There may be occasions when a bailiff will be in possession of a court order permitting forced entry, but all parties will generally be aware of that situation because the process will have gone through the courts. Goods may be removed by bailiffs or may sometimes be catalogued and marked and left in place with a prohibition on removing them. If the action arises because a rent is in arrears then goods that can be seized may include those that don't actually belong to the debtor, though the owner (who may have a retention of title right) may apply for their return.

The threat by a landlord of sending in the bailiffs makes it hard for the tenant to continue trading and therefore compromises the likelihood of the landlord receiving future rents. The landlord is therefore likely to try to avoid that situation and it may be possible to negotiate a deal with the landlord or the bailiff.

Negotiation is always preferable to either seizing goods or being on the receiving end and having them seized. That is because goods that are taken by bailiffs will usually be second-hand and the price they achieve at auction would be far lower than their replacement value. The bailiffs' fees are generally taken from the auction proceeds.

A company receiving a visit from bailiffs should always ask for identification and evidence of authorisation.

The ability of bailiffs to seize goods is suspended once a company registers with the courts its intention to apply for administration or obtains a moratorium in order to try to set up a Company Voluntary Arrangement (see below).

Debt recovery firms

Debt recovery firms offer a range of services, including sending letters to debtors, issuing court proceedings, recovering debts, providing a bailiff service and making seizures of property to pay bills. On the one hand their clients can write most of these letters themselves whilst on the other hand the impact is greater when it comes from a debt recovery company. The debtor is also concerned by the effect that a reference to a recovery company may have on their credit rating and hence on their ability to obtain credit in future.

Company Voluntary Arrangement

A Company Voluntary Arrangement (CVA) is a process for businesses that can persuade creditors and the courts that they are viable going forward, even if they cannot pay all their debts immediately. If they can persuade 75 per cent by value of creditors to support the proposal then all creditors are bound by it whether they voted for or against. The secured creditors, such as banks, retain their security and are outside the scheme. The unsecured creditors will typically agree to be repaid a percentage of their debts. The original directors remain in charge of the company but under the supervision of an insolvency practitioner who acts as supervisor until the CVA ends either as a result of the debtor discharging its agreed obligations or if it becomes clear it has failed. It must be noted that whilst this sort of procedure may save a business from failure it is also quite expensive; there is a need to pay fees to the supervisor as well as various court fees, so it will often not be suitable for very small businesses.

There is a procedure for companies to apply to the courts to obtain a short moratorium from their creditors whilst they try to put the CVA in place.

It is always worth considering, of course, whether to reach an informal arrangement with creditors. There may be instances where creditors may be prepared to accept a deferral of payment or a reduction in payment in the hope of getting some, at least, of their debt back. However difficult this may be to negotiate, it is always worth a business in difficulties considering it where there is a good prospect of future profitability and no substantial assets currently available for creditors to seize.

From the point of view of a creditor in this situation, it is usually best to seize assets but, if there are none available, perhaps because they are charged to a bank, then the option of trying to pursue an informal route to get some agreement for future payment should be considered; it too rarely is.

Court proceedings

If all else fails and one believes a customer can pay but won't, there is recourse to suing for redress. This is normally a straightforward procedure where a judgement is obtained; the case is usually undefended and is followed by a seizure of assets to pay the debt and costs. But if non-payment results from a dispute, rather than from a straightforward failure to pay an indisputable debt, then it is worth considering alternative dispute resolution procedures such as arbitration, mediation or, in some cases, an ombudsman scheme, which may all prove a lot quicker and cheaper. The problem with going through the court system in the event of a dispute is that it can be very expensive and risky: you may not win, in which case you may have to bear the other side's costs as well as your own. There are some institutions that will finance court cases for companies that cannot afford them, in return for a substantial share of the claim; however, they will generally only consider financing actions for large sums (over £1 million) and will require a legal opinion that there is a very high probability of winning.

The following example is not about recovery of a debt but illustrates some of the problems with pursuing legal actions.

Sales at one of our shops, located on the first floor of a shopping centre, plummeted when the landlords removed a passenger lift from outside it. We estimated our losses at over £100,000 per annum and commissioned an accountants' report to verify our figures. Their fees turned out to be much higher than we had agreed and our relationship with them was damaged when we refused to pay the extra. We tried to negotiate compensation directly with the landlord but to no avail: they did not respond. So, we appointed lawyers who were extremely dilatory but who commissioned, in turn, a legal opinion on the case, which was unsatisfactory because it did not address the crucial issues. So we refused to pay a part of that bill also and changed lawyers, moving to a larger, more prestigious and more expensive firm. Finally matters began to move forward: nearly two years had now elapsed from the removal of the lift and our sales remained depressed.

We obtained an opinion through our new lawyers that we had a good claim and a 60 per cent chance of winning. So we sent a notice of our intention to issue legal proceedings, which resulted in us finally beginning to have meetings with the landlord and their legal representatives. They denied that their actions had had the effect we claimed and argued that other factors had caused the sudden drop in sales. Their arguments were weak but they were delaying matters and our legal bills were escalating again. Our problem was that if we did issue legal proceedings then, from that point, we would be liable for the other side's costs if they won. Also, it was likely that the landlord would ask the court for security for costs in the event that they won. As a small company there was a risk that we might not be able to pay heavy costs, but we also could not easily find a deposit to pay into court whereas our opponents were a huge company that would clearly be able to pay any cost bill and therefore would not be asked to post security. Our counsel's estimate of a 60 per cent chance of winning did not seem high enough to make this look an attractive bet. We tried to look bigger and tougher than we really were and eventually managed to get an offer from the landlord to settle the case. The offer was worth around £60,000 and we had to pay our own costs of nearly £15,000, giving an outcome that was very low compared with our £850,000 claim.

The example illustrates that if there is an arguable rebuttal of your claim, then:

- **costs can make court action unattractive for all but the largest claims;**
- **trying to pursue a claim cheaply often leads to disputes over fees;**
- **a determined opponent, who can afford to do so, can create long delays and increase your costs.**

In some countries there are alternatives to the normal court procedures for small claims. In the UK, for example, there is a small claims system for claims valued at below £5,000, which operates through the courts but is much cheaper to pursue. It is often possible to manage the procedure without a lawyer and the proceedings can even be initiated online.

Cash forecasting

All businesses need cash forecasts. Those that have plenty of cash throughout the year and no significant calls upon it may only need a forecast in connection with annual budgets or questions of how much of the surplus can be invested elsewhere and for how long – those that have occasional shortages or major outgoings may require them monthly. In critical times when cash is very short you may need to carry out a very detailed cash forecast day-by-day so that you can deal with those problem times, such as when you have to pay rent and maybe service charges, your monthly supplier bills and wages, followed by the rates bill a few days later.

Whilst it sounds a big undertaking to have a daily cash forecast it is not really such an ordeal and, once it is set up on a spreadsheet it is easy to keep it updated, taking just a few minutes each day. Starting from today's date, put dates across the top. Then put your income categories down the left-hand side of the sheet and put in a total line. You will need to do a daily income forecast to drive this process. That is probably the hardest part because while costs are generally fairly easy to forecast – they are either the same each month or quarter or else they are a proportion of sales – sales tend to move around quite a lot and are quite unpredictable in most businesses, and so will need the most effort to produce a best guess. Remember that this is a cash forecast and therefore, having done a sales forecast, you need to add in a delay to account for when your customers will actually pay you. Also allow for the time it will take for the payments to be credited to your bank account so that you can draw on them.

Costs should be organised in categories and listed down the left-hand side of the spreadsheet below sales. The obvious categories of costs are:

- **stock purchases;**
- **staff costs;**
- **property costs;**
- **utilities, etc;**
- **other costs;**
- **taxes.**

If there are others that apply in your business then use them to help you capture all the important information and make it easier to understand. I suggest you sub-total each category and then have a total cost line at the bottom before the line for the cash movement for each day.

However, that is running ahead of myself. Having written down the categories so that you can understand what is going on, insert the names of individual suppliers under each cost category. This may make your spreadsheet very long but if you want the end result to be accurate there is no alternative. You can make the whole thing easier to follow by setting up a spreadsheet for each cost category that then feeds into the main spreadsheet, which will show the figures in aggregate. After that write down the amount you expect to pay each of the suppliers under the date you expect the payment to come out of your bank account (you can get these numbers from your accounting system). You can get an idea of payments going forward by looking at the pattern of payments in the past. When you don't know, put in your best guess. The accuracy of the cash forecast will probably deteriorate the further forward you look, but should be very good for three months. Use a minus sign for payments out and positive numbers for money coming in from your sales; see Table 4.1 as an example.

Table 4.1

	Wed 24 Sep	Thu 25 Sep	Fri 26 Sep	Sat 27 Sep	Sun 28 Sep	Mon 29 Sep	Tue 30 Sep	Wed 1 Oct	Thu 2 Oct
SALES	120	120	120	200	0	100	110	120	120
COSTS									
Supplier									
ABC bolts							−66		
BCD wrap							−34		
CDE tools		−25					−19		
Staff									
Wages							−350		
Taxes									−40
Property									
Rent								−500	
Taxes								−120	
Services								−95	
Other									
Utility A							−50		
EFG Stationery							−60		
Bank charges				−50					
Totals									
Daily cash	120	95	120	150	0	100	−69	−595	80
Bank balance	620	715	835	985	985	1085	616	21	101

In doing this exercise remember the importance of seasonality and of timing. Clearly, for a retailer, sales will be high at Christmas and payments high in February and March as suppliers are paid, but most businesses will have some seasonality. Remember the suppliers' individual credit terms and the practical point of when you actually do pay them. It may be your habit to stretch payments to some, so take that into account.

The month-end is important because for most businesses there is a payment cycle that is focused on the month-end. Take account of weekends and holidays because you won't issue payments then and bank accounts don't clear on those days. Actually, with increasing automated clearances there are occasions when payments do sometimes clear on a Sunday but usually these are for utility bills or other payments that are set up in advance on particular dates irrespective of the day. It is possible to take advantage of weekends when a month-end falls on one; issuing a payment just after the weekend can sometimes result in the payment not clearing from your bank account until after the following weekend. This is particularly useful when paying by cheque. You must then allow for the postal and the clearance delays. What matters is when the cash actually leaves your account.

If you are short of cash and you know that the credit controller you deal with at a significant supplier is on holiday, that may be the payment to delay a little. This can be risky if there is someone looking after your account in the interim who may be less understanding and just place all your orders on stop. In such circumstances your individual relationships will determine what you choose to do and it is always important to be aware of operational needs – don't delay payments to suppliers of time-critical goods or equipment!

Estimating recurring payments in the cash forecast can be done pretty accurately and fairly quickly by looking at past payments and timings from your bank statements and repeating them at the same times in ensuing months, adjusting for weekends and, where appropriate, the seasons. For example, most heating bills that relate to winter months will be much higher unless you use a budget account that smoothes out these differences.

This is a good place to summarise where you get data from to put this forecast together:

- **bank statements: primarily for regular payments to utilities, etc;**
- **sales accounts: for customer invoices already issued;**
- **purchase accounts: for supplier invoices already received;**
- **forecasts and budgets: particularly for sales going forward;**
- **management accounts: together with forecasts and budgets to assess future payments.**

Don't forget to enter tax payments and refunds. These items can be quite significant, though the dates may be hard to estimate accurately.

Get the closing bank balance for the night before you start this exercise and put it at the bottom at the far left of the spread sheet. At the bottom of your first column of workings you add the cash movement for the day to this balance and you have the closing bank balance for the first day. Use it as the opening balance for the next day and move the forecast as far forward as you feel is appropriate. Use bank statements as frequently as possible to look back at what actually happened to correct payments and receipts, and add in payments you had forgotten so that the actual figure at the foot of the forecast is correct for the past. This will continually correct your future forecasts.

Internet banking has made a significant contribution to improving forecasting and cash management since data are available daily. It has also made it much easier to switch funds between accounts and even to pay suppliers and be paid by customers easily and quickly. Since one can still pay a supplier by cheque if it is desirable to delay funds going out (postage and the paying-in process at the recipient can add two or three days) there is no real loss in flexibility. It is hard to think of a reason why any business would not use internet banking. Some banks do have better systems than others and it does make a difference if your bank takes a day longer to clear transactions: it is worth checking. We moved our account from a bank that transferred funds between accounts within minutes of receiving online instructions to one that made the transfer after the end of the business day. This meant that a transfer made on a Friday would not have effect until the following Tuesday – which pressured us to keep more money in a current account and less on deposit: good for the bank but bad for us. Similarly, banks that take longer to process payments in or out of accounts may also adversely affect their customers' cash flow.

To stop the forecast spreadsheet from becoming too big you will want to cut off the past history after a while. Do this by 'freezing' the last column or several columns, making sure that the brought forward bank balance at the close of business 'yesterday' is accurate.

The outcome of daily cash forecasting may show occasional days when there is an overdraft requirement that exceeds the available limit or, perhaps, where cash resources just seem a little lower than desirable – in case things turn out worse than forecast it is always wise to build a buffer into the target cash balance. It can be embarrassing if a supplier uses special cheque clearance to get their money before the weekend when you expected it to happen later. You then lose the advantage of using weekend trading or payments to pay the bill.

You have three options:

1. Try moving around costs, delaying payments where you feel you can.
2. Speak to your bankers to try to obtain larger overdraft facilities (perhaps only for a few days) or to raise money on invoices you have issued.
3. Change something in your business to cover the problem – dismiss staff, reduce stock levels, close premises, etc.

Whatever you do, do not just assume higher sales: hope is an unsafe way to address problems. Always tend to be cautious and understate your expected sales rather than being over-optimistic; this forecast is for you, not for the bank or an investor, and you really don't want to mislead yourself with false hopes. If you need to move around payment days there are several approaches you can use and they are discussed below under 'Supply'.

The process of cash forecasting should also be the time to consider uncertainties in cash coming in from customers. Look at your biggest customers and ask yourself, 'What would the effect be on me if they delayed payment for a week, maybe two, or even if they went bankrupt? What can I do to protect myself?' You can try to insure their debt with trade insurers; you can take a closer interest in their business so that you can form a faster opinion if they seem to be getting into difficulties. Is factoring of invoices an option? You can get regular updates on your customers from credit agencies. If there seems to be nothing you can do because you are very reliant upon one or two customers, then what about diversifying your business? Is that an option? Look for new opportunities and, if you can see any, can you put them into a separate company so that, if the worst happened, something would survive?

Releasing cash

You have cash tied up in three main places: property, stock and debtors.

Property

You may have a property you own and trade from. Do you need to own it or could you sell it and lease it back, or could you sell it and move somewhere else? If you examine your business plan and decide to do things differently, could you trade from smaller premises? What about sub-letting part of your space; does your lease allow you to do that? If you are not allowed to sub-let, might your landlord be persuaded to change this? Might your lease permit you to let someone in on licence, which is a very short-term rolling lease, where they take over space but they acquire no property rights and can be forced to leave on just a few days' notice?

Stock

Stock comes in three broad types: raw materials/components, work in progress, and finished goods. Do you need to keep so much by way of raw materials and components or could you organise more frequent replenishment and hold less? Maybe you could use a local supplier that can deliver quickly for some lines that you don't want to hold in stock. Can you speed up your production so that you have less work in progress?

Do you need to keep so much as finished goods? If you sell a number of products, do you need to keep the same level of finished stocks of all of them? Are there some lines you could hold less of or even make to order? Are you measuring how quickly your stock moves and do you have really slow-moving stock lines? If you do, what about selling them off cheaply and using the cash for faster-moving lines or just for the business generally?

Debtors

If you have debtors who owe you money you can chase them to pay more quickly, but there are debt factoring companies who will lend you money against them. This is getting harder as these lenders are increasingly nervous of debtors becoming bankrupt, but there are still such companies out there and it may be worth investigating, particularly if your customers are good quality and unlikely to fail to pay. Once again, use the internet – put 'invoice discounting' or 'factoring' into your search engine and go through the many options that will jump up.

Do you raise your invoices as quickly as you should? I know a consultancy business which, because it is the consultants delivering the services who also produce the invoices, tends to take a long time to invoice. The consultants focus on winning and delivering business but not so much on the dull chore of invoicing. Not many customers will pay you before you submit an invoice! Is there anything you can do to speed up the process of sending an invoice? Perhaps invoices can be automated more or someone else could produce them.

It is not unusual for customers to have one payment cycle at the end of each month – which means it is important to get goods out before each month-end so that they can be invoiced at the month-end and not during the following month. If necessary you could consider putting a month-end date on an invoice even if the goods are not despatched until after the month-end. You will soon find out which customers will accept this and which will object. Some customers will accept invoicing in advance on certain occasions, particularly at the end of their financial years, perhaps because unspent budgets will be set at a lower level the next year. Take advantage of this.

Invoice dates

If you frequently receive goods several days into a new month when the matching invoice is dated in the previous month, there is a case for refusing to accept this date and insisting on treating the invoice as being issued when the goods are received. It looks as though the supplier is trying to cut your credit period. Ideally you will get the agreement of the supplier to this or persuade them to change their practices rather than just taking unilateral action, but if needs must .... The precise date of sale can be quite complicated to establish and depends on the individual terms and conditions of each supplier. It can normally not be before the item is despatched and, in some cases, may be when delivered. If a supplier sent out goods and invoiced just before a long holiday, knowing that goods would sit in a distributor's warehouse for a week, there would be a strong case for arguing that the sale happened when the goods left their storage.

Looking at this from the other side, as a seller, you might want to get a few days or even a month's extra cash by invoicing in advance. Ideally you would do this with the customer's agreement, but in any event, if you need the cash, you should be aware of the opportunities and, indeed, be alive to the possibility of rushing deliveries out before the month-end. Many customers will have monthly payment cycles and so getting goods out and invoices issued before a month-end is really important.

5

Managing costs

Cost reduction

There are three ways of approaching cost reduction: a quick fix, continuous cost control, and reengineering the business.

A quick fix

If you have profit or cash problems you may need to cut costs quickly to improve profitability and cash flow and, in extreme cases, save a business. This approach is very common, and a good illustration of its limitations comes from the world of venture capital, where academic studies and individual examples show management buyouts achieving rapid profit growth that also quickly tails off and even goes into reverse. What is happening? The managers who lead the buyout are highly incentivised to achieve a very rapid payback to the investors and so they cut costs significantly. If it is such a good idea, you wonder why they could not do this when they worked for the previous owners of the businesses but the reason becomes clear as, after a while, at least some of the gains created by overhead reduction are reversed. Maybe not all but some of those overheads were there for a reason – they really did support the business – and sooner or later they will need to be put back. The evidence shows that the business managers receive their rewards after about three years from the buyout and overhead costs begin to rise again from that point.

Are there ways of cutting costs that have a permanent impact? I think there are two approaches: continuous cost control and reengineering the business.

Continuous cost control

All businesses should have an approach of continuous review of costs so that waste is always being eliminated. The cost of energy, telecoms or management of the car fleet should be looked at regularly, and not every 10 years. One should always be seeking value for money – it should be part of the DNA of a business. It should never be necessary or possible for senior management to send out an edict that headcount is to be reduced by 10 per cent, because every new hire should be considered necessary when it occurs and managers should always be asking themselves whether particular roles or entire functions provide value for money.

This is a process of continuous improvement where Japanese businesses, in particular, have been world leaders. They build the improvement approach into their annual planning round and their budgeting process; they use a cascade approach where the top managers give targets to the next layer in the business, who in turn produce detailed plans to achieve them and so on down the hierarchy, using teams rather than individuals at each level. The system depends upon a team approach and is not just about cost reduction but about process improvement.

Reengineering the business

The final approach to reducing cost levels is to examine a

business to find new ways of doing things. This is sometimes called 'business process reengineering'. It involves looking afresh, imagining the business did not exist and thinking through the most effective and cheapest way of putting it together.

Cost-cutting is seldom the answer to fundamental problems but good cost control will buy time to get things right. The business problem that is seldom given enough thought is the long-term effects of mistakes, which applies to costs too.

Suppose you set up a business and employ too many staff – you need 10 people but employ 12, which is not a big difference and you believe, initially, that it is necessary to have more people to deliver customer service that will make you stand out from the competitive crowd. Five years pass and the business is struggling – it needs extra cash to break free of its problems and move forward to a more successful formula that you are certain will work. Now, you reduce staff numbers by two and find little resulting detriment to the business. Imagine if you had had the cash that has been spent on those two unnecessary staff members – over five years this is a big number.

The money you do not have available that might have been there if you had not made a mistake long ago might have arisen from any one of a hundred different causes. Of course, some of the money saved might have been spent on other things before you eventually encounter a crisis – you may have paid the money out in higher wages, for instance – but the example illustrates how overspending on monthly and annual charges can build up, over a few years, and should focus attention on continuous cost control.

Review the business by area

Start with the big costs first and look at each area of your business:

- **Is it profitable?**
- **Does it generate cash?**

- **How much money is tied up in stocks, debtors or property?**
- **What are its future prospects?**
- **Does it make sense to shut it down?**

You may need an accountant to help with allocating costs between different business areas but, in principle, it is not hard. Table 5.1 sets the scene for an example where a business manufactures three products in a single factory but using different amounts of space and resources.

Table 5.1

£000	Product A	Product B	Product C
SALES	200	300	500
Direct costs – variable	–85	–120	–200
Direct overheads – variable	–30	–20	–20
CONTRIBUTION	85	160	280
Direct overheads – fixed	–20	–50	–70
Share of central costs	–90	–95	–165
PROFIT	–25	15	45

There are costs that are clearly directly related to each product and which are referred to as 'direct costs'. These include costs such as a dedicated sales team for each product but not the share of a business-wide sales team. Clearly these direct costs should be deducted from the sales figure to give a 'contribution' to overheads and profit.

But how do you treat the overheads of the business; do you allocate a share to each product? If we discontinued Product A, would we be better off in a time period of months not years? It is loss making, but it makes a contribution to fixed costs. If we stopped selling it, could we save the share of central costs? If we can, then we would be £5,000 better off; if not then £85,000 worse off.

Alternatively, would cutting out Product A allow us to bring in another product that would produce a higher contribution without increasing central costs? If so, that would be preferable. However, accounting systems on their own don't have a way to show these opportunity costs; alternatives must be treated as individual investments whose cash flows need to be assessed against a base case of continuing with Product A. The best an accounting system can do is to show clearly what the contribution to overheads is of each product, which costs are fixed and which variable.

In the example the shared costs have been allocated according to sales achieved. However, there might be a more scientific way to do this that relates to the use each product makes of the common services – so property costs could be allocated as a share of the space used, whilst the accounts department would still be on turnover. If that resulted in reallocating £30,000 from Product A to Product B, the whole comparison changes.

There is a strong argument not to allocate costs unless they would be saved if the product was discontinued. The example illustrates how the way information is presented affects the decisions made. It doesn't show how much cash is tied up as working capital in each area; that could also affect choices made.

Focus on the big costs first

We have started with whole areas of the business and your biggest costs, where reductions would bring you the greatest benefit. However, your biggest costs are presumably the ones you have thought of already. Look at them again. Is there another way of doing whatever you do that may be cheaper? Could you manufacture some component rather than buying it in, or vice versa?

Pause for a moment. You do not want to ruin a business through cost-cutting that inflicts greater damage on a business than the benefits to be gained from money saved. On the one hand you have accountants who are accused of looking at the numbers and not understanding the business; on the other there are the operational people who are accused of always wanting to offer a gold-plated service when this is not necessary, and of forgetting profit. The accountant will say that you can see the costs, they are real: they are here and now, whilst the potential growth is just that – potential. We have shown how waste may look small in a single year but how, over time, the effect may be significant, so knowing which view is correct is important. This is always an area of conflict and there are no simple answers for resolving them. Someone must make the decision.

If distribution is a big cost think about using your own vans or, if you use Royal Mail then look again at all its services – there may be a cheaper one. Postal services offer lower prices if you partially sort your mail yourself. There are also consolidators who sort your mail with other customers and then use Royal Mail for delivery but pay lower prices they negotiated in recognition of their large volumes. Even a reduction of a few percentage points on your bill may be a lot of money. Can you use a slower service that costs less and will the customers even notice?

There are some big costs that we imagine are unassailable, but they may not be. I learnt this lesson when I was in charge of IT for a large retailer. We were close to our main hardware supplier and believed we got a good deal. Then I saw a newspaper article that suggested that the finance scheme they provided, which allowed us to swap our equipment but keep the financing within the same broad scheme, was actually very expensive. I spent time working through our numbers in detail and realised that this was true – we were paying far too much. However, we were tied in to a leasing deal we had signed and there seemed no way out. So I had a big confrontation with the supplier's chief executive and I ranted and threatened to put the equipment out on the street: all very theatrical. Did I mean it? Well, many years have passed but yes, I meant it at the time. The point is not whether I am a good negotiator, or a lucky one. The point is that a large cost that seemed impossible to shift was greatly reduced because the supplier gave in and reduced our charges substantially. Look again at those large costs – maybe there is a way of reducing them.

Don't forget utilities. Electricity, gas and telephone costs are smaller for most of us but there are lots of deals out there and they change all the time. If you are a member of a trade association, it may have discount deals with certain suppliers; check this out. If your trade association does not have these deals set up, maybe you could suggest it does so. It is important to keep an easily accessible record of all agreements with utility companies, outlining the broad terms and, particularly, the notice period. Some utility agreements provide for notice to be given only in a specified period before the expiry of a contract and, if that period is missed it may be impossible to switch to another supplier for another year. It is also common for an existing supplier to be prepared to match a competing offer but only if the customer gives notice of termination. It is therefore good practice to give notice of termination as soon as any supply agreement permits and then to renegotiate.

Insurance is often a forgotten area for cost reduction. On the one hand it is important to review insurances regularly to make sure one is adequately covered and to ensure that changes have been properly recognised; on the other one needs to get competitive quotations for renewals to try to force down premiums.

I used a trusted insurance broker for our business insurance but, as our renewal date approached, our bank's insurance arm asked us to give them an opportunity to quote for the business. I was reluctant because I had a good relationship with our existing broker but, since the proposed renewal premium was large, I agreed. The outcome was a 25 per cent reduction in the premium which, relative to the size of our business, was substantial. Although I gave our existing broker the chance to requote he was only able to narrow the gap to 20 per cent and so, reluctantly, I switched. He was angry with me because he claimed he had gone out on a limb for me, provided high quality service and had sacrificed part of his commission. But the financial saving to us was large: what price friendship?

When forcing down costs it is important to consider the non-financial issues too. Cheap insurance where the insurer tries to avoid paying out claims is not cheap at all. It is also common for insurers to win business with a cheap quote and then to raise their premiums in subsequent years, so constant vigilance is required. Existing providers will rely on inertia and the perceived inconvenience to the customer of changing, and will always proclaim the benefits of an existing relationship. I remain unconvinced of the value of loyalty to suppliers and suspect the benefits are more imaginary than real.

Staff costs

For most businesses staff really matter. Whilst the old saying goes that nobody is irreplaceable, your staff are the business. They know how things are done and have hard-won skills, experience and contacts. However, for most businesses the cost of staff is a substantial proportion of total costs and, on the face of it, the easiest of those costs to cut. Although there is now extensive legislation to confer and protect employment rights and to stop rapacious employers from treating staff unfairly, businesses under pressure can still usually reduce staffing or benefits as long as they observe the rules. You will need to take legal advice. If you are a member of a trade association it probably offers telephone advice on employment law as one of the benefits of membership. If you are not a member of an association, joining one to get access to this advice may justify the annual fee. The other route to follow is to contact the UK government sponsored Advisory, Conciliation and Arbitration Service that offers free advice to both employers and employees.

Minimum wage

Most countries now have minimum wage legislation that applies to most workers, though there are exceptions. In the UK there are two minimum wage rates, with the lower one applying to workers between the ages of 18 and 22, which is intended to encourage businesses to take on and train young workers. Many companies don't take advantage of this lower rate even though they regularly take on younger workers who contribute less to the business until they are trained. It is always worth considering whether there is an opportunity and it is appropriate to have younger workers on a lower rate for a while, since the saving can be at an annualised rate of up to £2,000 a year.

Freezing and cutting wages

Of course you can't unilaterally change someone's contract, but if it is a case of lower wages or no job then you may find staff willing to agree. They are likely to want to see everyone take part – including bosses – and some promised reward if things improve, perhaps through a bonus scheme, may make it easier to sell.

Many workers in many industries expect wages to be frozen in a recession. If your industry is one of those and your business is either not doing very well or you expect it to deteriorate, don't think you have to increase wages every year: you don't. Maybe, here too, to compensate for a freeze, this is the year to bring in a bonus scheme if you don't have one or to increase one you already have, or to look into individual performance-related pay. This may be the year to tie pay in to the business performance.

Pay reviews

Just because you have normally reviewed pay on 1 January in the past does not mean you have to do this every year. If you are short of cash, cancel the review or give everyone a zero pay rise, or shift the date to another one later in the year. If unions are recognised in your business then this may all be more complicated since you may have signed agreements or may be confronted by organised unrest if you try to make changes. However, you should not adopt the mindset that the annual review is set in stone. If you have a unionised business then maybe you should talk to the members: you may find them more understanding than you expect.

Cutting hours

Have you thought about cutting your trading hours to save money? If you are a retailer open on a Sunday, would it be worthwhile stopping Sunday trading? How much profit do you make on that day? You may trade in a shopping centre that has Sunday opening as a requirement in your lease but, in this economic climate the landlord may be reluctant to take legal action or terminate your lease on this ground alone. You might also approach other traders to see if a concerted approach would be possible.

Some companies have provisions in contracts of employment that allow employers to reduce working hours either temporarily or permanently, or provide for a layoff if there is a shortage of work but, even if you do not have this in yours, you may still be able to persuade your staff to accept temporary short-time working on certain conditions.

If an employee is laid off and receives no wages or is put on short-time working and receives less than half a week's pay for four consecutive weeks (or for six non-consecutive weeks within a 13-week period) because of a shortage of work, then the employee can give a written notice that he or she intends to claim a redundancy payment. You should, in this event, seek professional advice.

Redundancy

Different countries have different rules on redundancy and the complexity of employment law is outside the scope of this book. However, if you believe you have more staff than you need, or if a

role is no longer necessary or there is an economic case to close a site, then it is sensible to consider reducing staff and investigating how you can go about it.
Broadly, the key issues to bear in mind are as follows.

Voluntary redundancy

An employer may offer staff the opportunity to apply for redundancy, which has the advantage of avoiding the risk of legal challenges. However, it has the obvious disadvantage that those who apply may be those most able to find another job and may be the people you least want to lose.

Employers must abide with agreements

There are probably just two types of relevant agreement to consider. The first is the particular contract of employment of each individual, remembering that the contract may also include precedents and, by reference, a staff handbook. The second relevant agreement would be any made with trade unions. Either may establish particular procedures to be followed and compensation to be paid.

Fair selection for redundancy

You must select people for redundancy on a fair and objective basis using criteria such as:

- **relevant skills and competence;**
- **disciplinary record;**
- **experience.**

You must not discriminate on the grounds of sex, sexual orientation, trade union membership, age, race, religion, etc and you must bear in mind that your decision may be challenged by an employee at a tribunal. So, whilst you can establish fair criteria and allocate weighting, fairly, to different measures to try to selectively make redundant your least valuable employees, you may not always find this works out as you want.

Consultation

If more than 20 employees are to be made redundant in the UK at a single site within a 90-day period then there is a legal requirement to give advance notice to the government and to consult employee representatives. There is, in any case, a requirement to consult employees affected by redundancy on why they have been selected and to consider alternatives to redundancy.

If you have to make staff redundant, the law requires you to pay their entitlement immediately. However, if the reason for redundancy is that cash is short, this may present a problem. You can try to negotiate with the people affected to pay their redundancy over a period; this is really a desperate measure but tough times call for tough measures and maybe you can afford to pay them a little more money to compensate. Of course they can always take you to an industrial tribunal and they will win, but since that process will take several months they may prefer to negotiate a deal that will pay them over, say, three months rather than going to a tribunal and being paid in six months' time.

Staff morale

If you are freezing or cutting wages or considering reducing staff numbers, you need to be aware of the effects on staff morale. This is not someone else's problem: the finance role cannot ignore it. People worry about their jobs and about the company's prospects. If their employer is cutting back, they see their prospects for career development and for getting involved in exciting projects disappearing, along with the income that they had counted on, which may cause future financial problems. People who spend their time worrying are not always able to give their full attention and all their creative energy to their work which, in turn, means those sales forecasts may not be achieved.

As an employer, many of these problems are well beyond your power to fix but there are sensible things you can do to try to reduce stress and maximise the focus on the business. Most of these are things that are good management practice at any time but today's stresses reinforce their importance:

- communicate;
- praise;
- encourage personal development.

Communicate

When times are difficult for a business it is very important to keep staff informed as far as possible. Whilst it is unlikely to be appropriate to communicate everything – you would not want to be talking about a redundancy programme, for example, whilst its details are being worked out – most businesses err on the side of not telling people enough. Some staff will have an idea that the business they work for is not flourishing and, even if they do not respond by seeking an alternative job they are very likely, even if unintentionally, to work less effectively if they are worried.

Praise

Some managers, some organisations and some cultures are better than others at giving staff feedback. One should always let people know if they have done a good job. Praise is far more effective than criticism for improving performance.

Encourage personal development

It is worth noting here how important it is to encourage the development of skills, which has a strong positive influence on staff morale. This relates both to 'hard skills' like proficiency in using a computer or other tools and to 'soft skills' such as negotiating, coaching or leadership.

Outsourcing

Outsourcing is the process of getting an outside contractor to perform some of the functions of an enterprise. All businesses outsource in the sense that we don't do everything ourselves: we hire in other people and organisations to perform some functions. We continue to do the things that we regard as core activities that are fundamental to the business and we outsource those activities that someone else can do more cheaply or more effectively. Sometimes we simply get someone else to do something because it is a distraction for us to do it in-house. For example, few businesses will cover their computer maintenance themselves, nor their software support; many businesses will get someone else to do their catering or their cleaning. These are obvious examples and there may be other activities that can be outsourced to the benefit of the business.

It is a good idea to identify the core activities and core skills of a business for planning purposes anyway, but start by listing these and, separately, list the activities that really are not core to the business. This may not be as simple to do as to say. On the one hand it is clear that property management is unlikely to be a core activity for, say, a retailer or a recruitment agency; on the other hand the things a Human Resource department does may seem non-core to these businesses but they may be most unwilling to outsource them. Clearly there is something else going on here that we need to consider. Other characteristics of things we don't want to outsource are how critical they are to our business success and how important knowledge of our organisation is to performing them effectively.

A small business may need to use an outside contractor to design and manage its website but then, as it grows and the website brings in more business, it can afford to hire its own manager and recognises the need to directly control an activity that has become mission-critical. This raises the question of whether you can manage an external provider effectively, because there is probably a trade-off between 'control' and cost-effectiveness and we may tend to like control even when it is not essential and costs a lot of money. If you outsource your warehouse operation you may achieve enormous economies of scale and access to expertise you cannot replicate, but you could feel you are losing customer contact. If you observe an increase in complaints, you need to decide whether to forego the financial benefits and bring the function in-house, or to improve management of the relationship with the external operator.

Another factor to consider is how big the business is and how fast it is growing. A stationer and printing company I knew used an external consultancy to provide HR support to an administrator it employed directly. The consultant was able to provide expert advice in areas where the administrator did not have the experience or knowledge, such as employment law, as well as skills-based expertise. As the business grew, the consultant provided training to the administrator and, in due course, the business was large enough for it to be more cost-effective to use the administrator in a full-time HR capacity and employed someone else to take on the administrative tasks. The consultant was still retained for some tasks such as acting as a business coach for the managing director. Advice on employment law matters was obtained from the company's trade association as a benefit of membership.

This shows that cost-effectiveness can vary as a business develops and as different services become available; it also shows that the needs of a business may call for different expertise at different times in its development. The example illustrates the need to look at different components of an activity as well as the overview; here some components of HR management were brought in-house but others remained outsourced. It is therefore clear that the different ways of performing tasks that are non-core to the business need to be reviewed regularly.

Remember also that just because a business is small, outsourcing is not the default position; it can work the other way too. Being involved in a small business I decided it was cheaper to learn enough about health and safety requirements to be able to produce the necessary policy document for the business myself, whereas if the business had been bigger I would probably have felt there were better uses of my time and got an outside firm to do it.

6

Supply

There are two key supply issues in any business: first, security of supply because nobody can trade without inputs; second, the cost of those inputs and the terms on which they must be paid.

Security of supply

What would you do if your main supplier failed? Suppose you are a retailer and it happened just before Christmas? This is not just fanciful; in 2008 the parent company of one of just two major book wholesalers went into administration at the end of November. In this case it looked as though the wholesale subsidiary would continue trading as usual, but if it didn't ... ? If you were in a similar situation, do you have a credit account with another wholesaler? Are your computer systems tied in to a wholesaler whose parent is in difficulty? If service deteriorated at this critical time would you be able to buy directly from the manufacturer? Do you have credit accounts set up? What about returns, if the company will not honour its, possibly unwritten, commitment to take back unsold stock after Christmas? In this particular case there were reports in the financial pages of the newspapers about the parent company for a long time, so it was possible to prepare some contingency plans.

What else could go wrong with people who supply you? Do you have a particular computer software supplier who maintains your systems and do you have a right to use that software in its absence? Do you know the home or personal mobile telephone number of someone who might maintain your systems? Suppose you use one of the computer systems that routes over the internet and through the supplier's computer servers: if those servers were not there, how quickly could you shift to another supplier?

Is there anyone else who is critical? You send items out by post through a consolidator, perhaps? If they were not there you could shift to Royal Mail, but what are the cost implications and how long would it take to set up an account?

Of course you cannot cover every possible disaster scenario but you can, at least, have thought about your options and what you would do if ....

Terms of trade

Your terms of trade are the prices you pay, the credit period you get and the amount of credit advanced. All of these are flexible; just because a price is on a price list does not mean there may not be a discount available.

If you don't ask you won't get

A recession is a good time to ask for better prices from your existing suppliers and to check what other suppliers may offer. If you don't ask you won't get. It is often worthwhile to try to find out what a new customer would be offered. Insurance is a good example of this. I found out that my insurers were offering new customers better rates, so I threatened to leave and got a better rate. I found exactly the same thing for our business electricity – the supplier would only match the competition if I threatened to leave. Another time I was outraged by the increase in my car insurance on renewal: when I protested I discovered that the person I was speaking to at the call centre had discretion to cut the price by 10 per cent.

Your suppliers will try to rely on your natural reluctance to switch and will take advantage of loyalty and any personal relationship you may have. When a salesperson visits you, gives you samples and buys you a coffee, he or she is trying to build a relationship that will retain your business and make you less likely to ask for a lower price. I remember the instance when a huge international computer supplier invited me, amongst its other customers, to its annual conference. It was interesting, informative and quite fun too. It gave little free gifts as well as wining and dining us. I was fairly new in the job and it was only a little later that I realised it was charging us a very hefty price. Our overall bill was £400,000 per year and I eventually got it down by £100,000. I didn't get invited to any more of those events, but £100,000 can pay for a lot of free diaries.

There are many different ways of setting a price: there is the headline price on the price list, discounts are available for volume, or deals can be struck because the supplier is afraid of losing your business.

Don't push too far

Only you can judge how far to push your suppliers. I am afraid this is an art and not a science. Ask yourself whether this is a one-off transaction or a continuing relationship. If it is a one-off then you have much more scope to be hard-nosed.

I was told a story by someone who visited a jewellery shop run by their cousin. The cousin was selling a wedding ring to a young man and his father. It was clear they liked the ring but the conversation suddenly turned to price, with the customer asking what the jeweller could do about it. The jeweller offered a very small discount and then dug his heels in, saying he was already making only a small profit. In the end that was the price and the customer agreed. The cousin remarked, after the customers left, that since they had made no attempt to leave during the negotiation it was obvious to him that they were going to agree and he had no need to reduce the price further.

Ask yourself whether there is another identical product next door. Clearly, if there is an open, transparent market and lots of alternatives then you can play off one supplier against another and get the lowest possible price. However, in most cases there are differences between products and what you need to buy includes intangible elements such as the reliability of the supplier and the quality of service and, don't forget, the cost and trouble of going backwards and forwards between possible suppliers to negotiate the best terms.

There is some benefit to a relationship and, if you sour yours, the supplier may not help you out when you need it. You may suddenly find that you need a very quick delivery which requires them to work a bit harder and put themselves out, and they may not be so keen after you have had an argument about price. They may also reduce the quality of supply if you cut too hard. A good analogy is the builder who cuts corners because you have cut the price so deep that he is barely making a profit. However, my experience is that 'relationships' are overdone; they often seem to be one-way things. Our computer supplier in the example I gave above continued to supply us, though I expect it looked for other ways of charging us more. I have found that builders often try to cut corners whether or not you get their price down. Overall, I believe that relationships are mended fairly quickly and that if your suppliers think you are a good enough customer, they will agree to your lower price and will not antagonise you by being uncooperative when you need their help. Still, the final judgement is yours.

If there is more than one person in the business who can negotiate with suppliers it is sometimes a good idea to have one of you as the nice guy and the other as the nasty guy. If it comes to asking for a favour in future, the nice guy may find it easier.

Extending payment terms

You can always try to extend payment terms on a formal basis. Too few businesses try to do this and, of course, it is hard. The supplier has to find extra working capital to fund the delay. Information is key here: the more you can find out about other customers' payment terms the stronger your negotiation can be.

Which organisations due payment can be delayed for a few days if necessary? The first obvious one is the government, but that can raise some problems. You are due on the 19th of the month to pay over National Insurance and PAYE tax that you have deducted from employee wages at the previous month-end. You can always delay your cheque for a few days, but if you do this for month after month you will start getting telephone calls from the tax authorities. They can be quite unpleasant and threatening; they can also send people in to your premises to collect a cheque and in the last resort they can send in bailiffs to seize your goods. If you only delay payment occasionally the authorities may be a little more understanding or, at least, not take action until you have achieved your objective of delaying long enough to get in a bit more cash to pay the bill. Do you tell the caller from HMRC that you have cash flow problems and need some time to pay? That depends on the individual who calls – if he or she feels you are on the edge of insolvency he or she may rush in to get some money, but it is more likely that a payment schedule can be agreed. There is a second disadvantage to this step. Suppose you manage to delay payment for a month or even two and then, unfortunately, the business still becomes insolvent despite your tactics. The authorities could seek to get the directors personally to pay the outstanding National Insurance and PAYE taxes. This is rare and usually happens only if the directors have acted improperly, but it is still a risk. If, for example, the tax payments have grown to four or five months overdue and the liquidator's report is critical of the directors, the risk to them personally could be very real.

What about your business suppliers? One of the most difficult questions, if you are short of cash to pay bills, is what to tell the suppliers. Do you tell them that you have a problem? They may respond sympathetically, or one or more could become more insistent, send in the bailiffs, issue court proceedings or stop supplying you. If the cash embarrassment is a one-off then the decision is easy – you can tell one or more of the suppliers that you need a little extra time to pay and, being assured it is a one-off, they are pretty unlikely to react badly and will appreciate that you told them. If the cash embarrassment requires a long delay in payment then you may be forced to tell the suppliers you have a problem because they will find out anyway and may be more upset that you did not keep them informed. If you have one or only a small number of significant suppliers you may be able to negotiate a special repayment schedule that carries you past your problem dates. A substantial supplier will be keen to retain your business and help you through if they believe that you will get through a short-lived problem period and resume business as usual. They are most likely to be helpful if you are an important customer to them – if you are insignificant then there is a much greater chance that they will be unhelpful because it is not worth the trouble or the risk.

If your difficulty is likely to continue for a while then you will probably need to delay payments to a range of people at each month-end. Landlords will usually put up with a few days of delay but, as with PAYE and NI, they do have draconian rights if they want to be difficult. The landlord has the right to send in bailiffs without warning to seize goods to sell and pay off your arrears. In practice very few landlords do this – they usually threaten first. National Insurance and PAYE can also be delayed, subject to the risks outlined above. Your creditors such as landlords and tax authorities will become more aggressive if it becomes a habit that every month or every quarter you pay late. To balance this, landlords may be concerned that they will not be able to find another tenant; perhaps the property is of poor quality or in a poor position, or the economy is going through a downturn, so they are more likely to compromise a little.

If your cash forecasts show a difficulty that seems to have no end then you may have a different type of problem that needs dealing with in another way. If the business is loss making or just does not have enough cash then you run the risk of trading whilst insolvent. Directors of limited liability companies are personally liable for the debts of a company if trading continues after there is no longer any reasonable prospect of avoiding insolvency. The issue is what a reasonable prospect is, and the risk is small if you could present a case that you were doing things that you reasonably believed had a good chance of resolving your problems. If a company becomes insolvent then the administrator or liquidator is charged with reporting upon the conduct of directors. If this report suggests misconduct, the directors may be disqualified from acting as directors and can be open to legal action by creditors who lose money. Therefore, if managing cash better for a while will not resolve the problem your choices are likely to be:

- **sell the business;**
- **call in an administrator;**
- **find someone to invest more money;**
- **find a radical change to your way of trading.**

Raising queries

Of course it is often possible to create cover for delaying a payment by raising a query, whether disputing the delivery date or claiming an imperfection or incompleteness. However, this is not the sort of stratagem that bears much repetition: a bit like the claim that 'the cheque is in the post' it can lead to disbelief and its consequences. On the other hand, if the query happens to be honest and true then withholding payment is often remarkably effective in influencing a resolution.

Deal with people at the right level

A former colleague of mine was always more comfortable dealing with less sophisticated people. Although he could boast the title of managing director of our small organisation he nonetheless drifted down to dealing with the sales managers rather than the bosses. Sometimes that is the right thing to do: often the sales director will be more restrictive and his or her subordinates more accommodating, but in tough times be sure you are dealing with the decision maker who has authority to give you the best deal and not with someone who has to refer up the hierarchy. Always connect with people at the highest level you can.

Stock clearances

It may be just the right time to see whether your main suppliers, or even not so main ones, may wish to turn some of their old stocks into cash. If you have the funds to be able to buy more than you need in advance, or if you have an idea to sell on quickly, then there is always an opportunity for the nimble-footed. With the increasing number of channels to market in many industries, companies are sometimes willing to clear stock through one of them in the belief that it will not affect prices in others. This is obviously untrue but belief by others in false ideas can always provide a profitable opportunity. A good example of this is the book trade, where publishers sell to wholesalers, to retailers, to book clubs, to direct sellers, directly to customers and to dealers. The dealers will sell on to second-hand shops and to internet traders. Prices to these various segments differ enormously so that if you are a retailer but can buy as a dealer then you can make a large extra profit. The same will apply in many industries: you can seek out end-of-line goods that the supplier wants to clear and you can switch the segment you are allocated to so that you buy at a larger discount than would normally be the case. In bookselling a well known retailer managed to buy at wholesale prices for years and made large extra profits as a result. The international clothing chain TK Maxx has built its entire business on buying last season's end-of-line products at a discount and selling them on. Clearly there are trade-offs such as the risk of buying unfashionable stock that will not sell at any price or, in computing, outdated computers that will inevitably be harder to shift through some markets.

Credit ratings

Many suppliers will use credit insurance and, if times are tough, this can be a problem. The insurer may analyse your accounts and reduce your credit rating. If you produce annual accounts, you may want to delay sending them in to Companies House for as long as legally possible, perhaps until the next year's figures show a better picture.

All countries have deadlines for the filing of accounts. In the UK there is a requirement to file accounts within 22 months of the formation of a company and within 10 months (nine months for companies formed after 6 April 2008). The fines for late submission are now quite substantial: £150 for up to one month, rising to £1,500 for more than six months. If there is also a late filing the following year, that year's scale fine is doubled. Although there is a procedure for applying for an extension, this is only granted in exceptional circumstances where a significant event has occurred to the company.

Depending upon the insurer you may be able to appeal to them, explain your business and get them to reconsider the rating they give you and the cover they will extend. If this is not possible you can appeal directly to your supplier to supply you outside the terms of their insurance. The alternative, if your credit is reduced, would be to pay the account more frequently which, of course, requires more working capital to compensate for the reduced credit.

7

Property

Rent

Property costs are usually seen as unchangeable once you have signed a lease, and that is certainly usually true. However, it is still worth thinking about. If there are a lot of empty properties in your vicinity then your landlords may be willing to consider something such as a reduced rent now in exchange for a higher rent in a couple of years' time or in exchange for a longer lease. They may consider this if they are convinced that you will go out of business if they don't agree or, conversely, if they are convinced you will stay in business and the higher rent in two years' time is a substantially bigger increase than the sacrifice they must make now. Because commercial properties are valued on the basis of the rent they bring in, a landlord may be resistant to changing the headline rent but may agree a 'side deal' that need not be notified to the Land Registry. Whether, as a tenant, one agrees to this approach depends upon one's negotiating position but it is fraught with risk. How binding is a side deal, and what happens if the lease is sold by the landlords or if they cease to trade?

If you are taking new premises then you need to assess how keen the landlords are to have them occupied and what competition you have. How many empty premises are there in the vicinity?

In times when property has been hard to let landlords have offered deals to give the tenant an up-front payment, which is referred to as a 'reverse premium' and may be used to pay for fitting out premises. The accounting standards require this to be shown in the P&L over the period of years to the first rent review. This is to avoid the abuses of the past when large retailers, in particular, would treat such premiums as trading income in the year it is received, which could mislead users of their accounts into thinking the underlying business more profitable than it was. In the worst cases the tenants would actually pay higher rents in later years in order to get a higher premium, which is a form of hidden borrowing as well as a distortion of the profits. Conversely, when properties have been hard to find or a tenant is assigning a lease with a low rent, there may be a premium to pay by the tenant.

Be careful about stepped rent deals. If you are offered a low rent now but a rising rent later, do consider whether that final rent is expensive; your next rent review will take that high figure as its starting point. You may be able to agree a rent review based upon the average rent over the period, but that is unusual. Not only will that final rent be high, but when the Valuation Office sets your next business rates the rent you pay will be taken into account.

Withholding rent can be a very dangerous but effective negotiating tool. Some landlords will play tough and be outraged if you delay or withhold rent, and they have the power to send in bailiffs to seize goods. On the other hand, if you really do have financial problems then you may think you have little to lose and you can always pay up if you have to.

If your landlords have financial problems

If you have a formal lease on the property then you don't need to worry about your landlords' financial position. However, if you have a short-term tenancy agreement outside the Landlord and Tenant Act you may be affected by their problems. This is an issue if they don't pay their mortgage and the lender sends in bailiffs. The lender is meant to give the occupier five weeks' notice, so do make sure that you check all mail that is addressed to 'The Occupier' or even to both 'Landlord and Occupier'.

Sub-letting

Most commercial leases will prevent sub-letting without the landlords' consent but you can, of course, seek their consent. The alternative is to see if you can grant a licence to someone else for space you no longer need. This is a short-term agreement that confers fewer rights but, for instance, is often used by retailers to allow 'implants' in their stores by other retailers. In that case the other retailer may use the same cash tills as the prime occupier and trading proceeds are split between them. Landlords tend to be less concerned with licences since they confer no property rights on the licensee, but the landlords must still give permission. Depending upon the space you occupy and whether it can be securely subdivided, you may be able to persuade a landlord to take back some surplus space you no longer need.

Service charges

Service charges levied on lessees can be a really contentious area with big landlords, particularly in large developments with multiple occupancy. The lease will define the landlords' rights to recover money spent on the upkeep of the properties and they will generally have no incentive to minimise the service charge: they want the estate to be in the best possible condition and if they are inept and waste money then your rights will be limited. Nonetheless, never just accept that you must pay up. Check your lease and see what your rights are. Try to have a good relationship with your landlords and their local managers in good times; ensure there is a tenants association and attend meetings; keep in touch with other tenants and complain forcefully if things go wrong. Very large landlords may subscribe to a code of practice, such as exists in the UK – it is worth checking if yours do.

We had a shop in a large shopping centre and a new landlord started raising the service charge; new staff were appointed, repairs and new equipment escalated and the cost fell on the tenants. There were new marketing expenditures and consultants retained – all to little effect – and again, the cost fell on the tenants. We felt the additional expenditure was badly allocated, in part supporting the landlord's central organisation that served all of the shopping centres it owned.

We wrote to all the tenants, copying the landlord's managers and protested forcefully – we succeeded in getting a tenants meeting with the landlord. We tried to get the big space users, which paid the largest part of the charge for the whole building, to take the lead. We also withheld a part of the service charge. This could have caused us problems according to the strict terms of the lease, but by insisting we were disputing the bills we managed to escape recovery processes whilst exerting pressure on the landlord.

In our case, despite everything, we failed to get anywhere because the big space users, who had most leverage, could not be persuaded to take a strong enough line. Whilst it is possible to challenge a landlord's claims for service charges through the courts, this is an expensive process, which benefits from having large companies joining the protest. Nonetheless, this is a cost area that should not just be accepted as unchallengeable.

Business rates

Local business taxes can be paid by monthly instalments in the UK but failure to pay on time may provoke the authorities into demanding the whole outstanding amount forthwith. If you are unable to pay they will send in bailiffs to seize goods to the value of the debt. Depending upon the Council, they may be more or less understanding and helpful. You may be able to arrange for a new payment schedule, so it is always worth talking to them, but it is a fine line between persuading them you can pay but need a little time, and not being able to pay at all. If you can't pay at all they may as well send in the bailiffs and get what they can.

Small business rates

Since 1 April 2005 rate relief has been available for businesses in England occupying a property with a rateable value below £10,000. Up to and including a rateable value of £5,000 the discount is 50 per cent and between £5,001 and £10,000 the relief will fall 1 per cent for every £100 in value. If a business occupies several properties, the total rateable value must be below £10,000. The relief must be claimed within six months of the end of the chargeable year.

If your business could qualify for this relief it is also worth considering whether there may be grounds for a rating valuation appeal. A number of firms that carry out such appeals will work for a fee based on a percentage of the reduction in valuation they obtain and will never, in my experience, cost more than the first year's saving.

Empty property rates

The UK government drastically reduced the rate relief available on empty business properties in April 2008, but there has been a considerable outcry against this, so it is worthwhile keeping an eye on the situation. Relief is currently available at 100 per cent for six months for industrial properties and for three months for other commercial properties.

After this time the only way to escape rates will be to render the buildings unfit for occupation by action such as full or partial demolition. Do note that advice may need to be taken on this as removing the roof, for example, may not be viewed as sufficient.

8

Buying undervalued assets

When you buy new assets for a business they are usually significant purchases in the context of the enterprise and getting a good deal is important. It is therefore worth putting considerable effort into acquiring assets at a good price and achieving the best possible deal.

Some asset deals are readily available from familiar suppliers –you just need to ask – some need seeking out. We often buy from the people we have always bought from or those recommended by friends and colleagues. What about foreign suppliers? They may not be on the spot to deal with potential problems, an issue few buyers think through. Perhaps retention of part of the price to cover eventualities, or being assured that local support will be available, will overcome any doubts.

I invested in computer software supplied by a company in a wholly different time zone, eight hours removed from mine. This was a business-critical purchase and it turned out there were support issues arising from the time difference and also from a different pattern of national holidays. Somehow things always went wrong when support staff were unavailable and when I could reach them it meant staying at work well into the evening to resolve the problem. However, on balance, these inconveniences did not outweigh the benefits arising from this particular software so we persevered.

What about trading down? Do you actually need the level of quality that you pay for or would a lesser product be perfectly acceptable?

These asset purchases are usually one-off purchases, even if there may be a string of them over time, which means you may not be dealing with the seller again in the short term, may not have a continuing relationship and therefore can be more aggressive to achieve what you want. Negotiation is a crucial tool in every aspect of business but never more so than when acquiring assets for the business.

Negotiating the best deal

There are a few basic negotiating ideas that need to be part of the armoury of effective financial management:

1. establish objectives in advance: the middle of a negotiation is not the time to be working through what one wants to achieve;
2. preparation is essential: the cliché that 'failing to prepare is preparing to fail' is actually true;
3. a win-win result is possible: some find it hard to accept that both sides can win but they can;
4. negotiation is trading: there may be things that have less value to you than to them that you can trade to get what you want;
5. listen: active listening involves asking good questions and not just hearing the response but analysing and understanding it and seeking mutual benefits;
6. if you don't ask you won't get.

Much of business is about negotiating, so one should approach any purchase, any sale, and any contract taken on as an opportunity to improve on the deal being offered. That does not have to mean being constantly aggressive and alienating everyone; there really are opportunities to find a deal that is better for everyone and without being unpleasant. Point 6 in the list above bears repetition: if you don't ask you won't get. There are many occasions when I have asked for a better price or an upgrade or a variation on what is being offered and even I have been surprised how easily it is conceded.

Buying in a bankruptcy

Nowadays the process of bankruptcy is usually referred to as 'administration' rather than 'receivership'. Administrators will try to sell assets to ensure the creditors are paid as quickly as possible, and be unwilling to offer guarantees of any sort about the quality of the assets you are buying. The business in administration will not be in any position to give any guarantees and the administrators will not take on that responsibility. You must examine the assets they are selling yourself and check they are as you expect. If you have concerns about the risk of failure then withhold some of the price and arrange stage payments.

The administrators must not be seen to sell assets at an undervalued price but it is a fact that the assets of a business fall in value the moment it goes into administration and therefore they often want to achieve a quick sale. In some cases where assets are hard to sell you may even find that administrators will finance your purchase by giving you time to pay, which means you can buy stock with only a down-payment and then sell it and use the proceeds to pay the purchase price. A similar thing can happen when part of a business is closed down by a parent company but the rest of it continues to trade. If the closed business interests you, check whether there could be product guarantees that the parent is still responsible for. If there are then they may be very anxious for someone else to take them on and fulfil them.

A successful but low technology engineering company took over a hi-tech business that was in trouble, for a very low price. Things went ok for the first year but then deteriorated, and after another couple of years they decided to cut their losses and close it. However, they had sold equipment around the world to large businesses and the parent company, which continued to trade, was responsible for repairs under warranty. They did not want to continue providing this service but were frightened that a large customer might take action through the courts if they found they had equipment that would not work because of a backlog of repairs. So the management of the hi-tech business were able to buy all its know-how and stocks of parts for £1.

The other side of this coin is that a company selling a part of its business may seek to get the buyer to shoulder responsibilities that neither the seller nor buyer wants. Be very careful about what you buy. Try to buy assets rather than a company because the company may have hidden liabilities and, whilst it is good if you can get the seller to guarantee there aren't any, such liabilities could surface later and your guarantor could be declared bankrupt or just can't pay or won't cooperate and you can't afford to take the matter to court. You can buy a trading name or know-how without buying a company: you can also take on staff without the company. If you take on most of the staff they will probably still preserve all their employment rights as if they were still working for the original employer, under the TUPE (Transfer of Undertakings (Protection of Employment)) regulations.

If a competitor closes you may be able to buy its customer lists even if you don't want the whole business or the assets. If this is an attractive idea, or you want to buy more of its assets, keep your ear to the ground and respond quickly if you hear of a competitor that may be in trouble. For the sake of a quick telephone call you may get a bargain. If the rumour was wrong the worst that can happen is that you will be slightly embarrassed by the telephone call.

A friend of mine established a medical business shortly after a competitor with a different business model fell into administration. He was able to ring the company and its administrators and buy equipment for less than 20 per cent of its price when new (purchased just a few months earlier), to get other equipment without charge and to obtain customer lists for nothing.

When a business fails there may be a certain amount of chaos with people not quite knowing what to do and what they are allowed to do. The administrator wants a quick result and needs to repay secured creditors such as the bank. It could be that in this case the bank credit was secured by personal guarantees and that, as far as the administrator was concerned, having a buyer ring up with an offer of 20 per cent of the cost of equipment without the expense of advertising and paying commissions was a lucky blessing. The person who let the customer list go probably thought there were no other potential buyers and it was not worth the trouble of negotiating a price that would, anyway, disappear in fees.

Buy second-hand and from the internet

You probably wouldn't normally buy things second-hand but there are a host of things that are available more cheaply. Computers are a prime example and the prices can be very attractive. Many buyers from larger businesses will feel that they need the comfort of knowing they buy from original equipment manufacturers or their dealers so that there is a support network and helpdesk in place, particularly when it comes to buying computers. You can buy a new computer that is an old model or that is second-hand at a small fraction of the price you would pay for a new one. If cash is tight and you back up frequently then this may be ideal for you. There are companies that will provide support on any equipment and if a system is properly backed up, and the price is attractive, why not be prepared to throw out equipment that fails and plug in a replacement? Computers last much longer than they used to: the limiting factor is usually that after about three years they become outdated and will not run the latest software. As well as visiting trade fairs or small computer shops to see what's available, you will find lots of companies advertising on the internet by searching for 'computers end of line'. Some of these will have some form of guarantee available even if only for a limited period.

It is possible to find a whole host of other fixtures and equipment available through dealers. It is also worth looking on eBay. Items like lighting and shelving and more sophisticated equipment is often available cheaply as bankrupt stock, under the internet search term 'liquidation', or through the trade press.

Buying cooperatives

Trade associations are in many ways a form of buying cooperative. Of course they also lobby on behalf of their members and may provide training courses and run exhibitions, they may even provide professional qualifications; nonetheless, a major attraction of membership is that they provide cheaper bulk-buying opportunities. Consider, as an example, the British Shops and Stores Association; this provides discounts on credit card charges, banking, insurance, rating reviews and telecoms as well as free telephone legal advice and advice on health and safety requirements. It is well worth investigating bodies such as this that you may be able to join. Don't forget cash and carry companies such as Costco that you may be able to use personally as well as for business.

9

Banks and borrowing

When trading is tough, the old adage about banks comes true: 'They lend you an umbrella when it's dry and want it back when it rains.' To be fair, the bank is tight on funds in such times and has to get back its cash somehow. In addition, banks see asset prices falling and risks increasing so they seek personal guarantees. Most bank loans as well as personal mortgages will have a clause permitting the lender to call back the loan at any time. Usually this is not an issue, but when the lender demands repayment within 30 days during a credit crunch then you have a problem. There are regular reports in the newspapers of banks doing just that on personal mortgages that they have issued at very attractive rates when they suddenly look ridiculously cheap.

What can you do? You can make a big fuss. Banks do not like that and it will not endear you to them but, if you are in a real bind, what do you care? Contact your parliamentary representative, complain to the Financial Services Authority, contact the press and see if they are interested, try consumer programmes on TV and radio, use your trade bodies to complain and protest. Look for another bank. You will need to be able to show them a business plan, which I have covered elsewhere in this book – don't just walk in to see a prospective new bank manager, or even an old one, with a few ideas in your head – show them a convincing written plan.

If you have a good business or a good business idea you can try to raise money from traditional sources such as family and friends (see below). You can ensure you have facilities in place that are not 'on demand'; a term loan is harder for the bank to withdraw suddenly. Make sure you have some sort of relationship with more than one bank, keep the bank informed and tell a good story. Unless your trading is so bad that you don't want the bank to know, provide them with monthly figures and forecasts to persuade them not to withdraw facilities from a good business. Avoid exceeding your overdraft – make your creditors finance you if necessary.

Personal guarantees

In the UK, and in some other countries, it is quite common for a bank to ask for personal guarantees from directors to secure a loan. This, of course, strips away the protection of having a limited liability company but may be unavoidable. It means that, if the business fails and there are insufficient assets to repay the bank, directors risk losing their investment, their job and personal assets too. Since such guarantees are joint and several, the bank will probably pursue the directors who have the most easily identifiable assets rather than the most culpable, and may also choose to pursue only one, leaving others alone. Nonetheless, it is always worth negotiating – in my own business we obtained a substantial loan without having to give such a guarantee. If it proves impossible to avoid giving a guarantee it may be possible to limit it in time, to have it discharged if the outstanding loan falls below an agreed figure, or to have it secured only on specified assets. Of course the bank officials will try to avoid any limitation and, if they do agree, will want to avoid giving anything in writing. The directors, on the other hand, should try to have any such agreement included in the legal documentation of the loan or, at least, evidenced in a letter from the bank.

Managing your banking relationships

Your relationship with your bank is very important both because it may be lending you money and because it manages your day-to-day transactions. Despite the shift towards impersonal, internet banking these transactions will go wrong every once in a while and you will need human intervention to help you out. Having a bank manager who you know reasonably well will help in getting them to resolve problems with another department of the bank where you may not have any personal relationship.

Banks adopt two different approaches to customers: building relationships and focusing on transactions. This means that if a business has a problem and needs help – for instance it has a borrowing limit and expects to exceed it for two days – the manager who adopts a relationship approach may allow some excess borrowing for a short period, knowing that the business has always warned when such short-term problems have arisen in the past and they have not turned into long-term ones.

Bank managers don't like surprises. Generally they are willing to be flexible if they have some advance warning of a problem but far more reluctant to do so when confronted with an unexpected turn of events. So usually it is best to keep your lender informed, even if you may put the most optimistic interpretation on outcomes. This means that you should supply regular accounts in a timely manner if that has been agreed, and you should call your contact manager from time to time if he or she doesn't call you.

Bank managers don't like to lose money. This seems to be stating the obvious but it is more subtle than it seems. Imagine that a bank borrows at 5 per cent and lends to you at 7.5 per cent; its contribution to costs and profit is 2.5 per cent. Suppose the contribution to their overhead and operating costs is 1 per cent, leaving 1.5 per cent of profit. That means that over 60 years of interest on borrowing are required to compensate if your business fails and the bank loses the money it lent you. This is reflected in banks' internal control systems where staff are judged on how much money they have lost just as much as how much money they have made. The implication of this is that if your business has a really serious risk of loss to the bank it is usually best not to reveal quite how bad it is for as long as possible. At the point where a bank loan is classified as 'at risk', responsibility may be transferred to a recoveries team who may have less discretion.

Make sure you are dealing with people at the right level and in the right department. There is no point in continuing to discuss your issues with the bank manager you have a good relationship with if responsibility has moved to a recoveries team and is out of his or her hands. Similarly, you need to be speaking to the most senior manager you can because you are more likely to be dealing with the decision maker. I have had experience of a bank manager being rather panicky and closing a trading account, which caused immediate trading problems with credit card terminals no longer working; a more senior manager might well have been persuaded to keep it open for paying money in, at least, and it would have been much easier to continue trading.

Review your agreements

Do you have a formal written agreement with your bank? If you do, make sure you know what it says. Can it withdraw your overdraft at any time; are you meant to provide monthly accounts; should there be an annual review? I sort of forgot those monthly accounts when business was not too good and the bank forgot to ask. That was useful in the short term but, as events caught up with us, it suddenly put us under a lot of pressure to produce accounts in a hurry.

If there is an agreement, are there conditions you are meant to observe, such as not making trading losses or borrowing representing a specified percentage of shareholders' funds? A loss in one year can cause mayhem with borrowing ratios. Depending upon the agreement, you may want to get a formal waiver from the bank if you breach one of these undertakings (also referred to as 'covenants'). That might prevent the bank from converting a term-loan into a call-loan, which gives it the right to call for repayment of the loan with little or no notice.

Except for term loans that define a schedule of repayments, most loans are 'on call' and can be withdrawn at any time. This also means that the terms of the loan can be changed at any time.

After 14 years of trading our bank suddenly demanded that we give directors' guarantees on our loan. Since we were not prepared to do this it meant that, with only a month's notice, we had to repay the loan. To be fair to the bank, our trading had deteriorated in a difficult climate. However, the point is that borrowers need to understand what their bank can do and to be aware that credit shortages have happened many times over the years. The best defences are to have a good relationship with the bank, to keep it informed of trading progress and to have long-term borrowing funded by a term loan so that its conditions cannot be changed overnight. An overdraft or any other form of on-demand loan should only be used to finance short-term, fluctuating requirements.

Refinancing

In more stressful times when the availability of credit has shrunk it can be hard to get loans or leasing. However, at the same time, interest rates will have fallen so it is a good time to see if you can find a lender who will charge you less. See what the availability is of fixed rates that are lower than you are paying at present. You may even find that your current lender is willing to refinance over a longer period at a lower rate. Even though there may be charges and penalties payable for early repayment of a term loan, it is worth reviewing the figures regularly to check whether this option makes sense.

In normal times a business that is a bit short of cash would be recommended to consider refinancing over a longer period or at a lower interest rate as a means of releasing cash. That will be far harder for a struggling company than for one that is doing well, and also is more difficult in periods when credit is tight, but it is still a step worth investigating.

Businesses occasionally use credit card debt as a longer-term means of borrowing. This is very expensive and should only be used as a last option. The rates charged by the credit card companies do not fall by much in downturns even though interest rates on other forms of borrowing fall substantially.

Leasing

In harsh times the attractions of leasing equipment and cars may be even greater but is worth consideration at any time. Perhaps you would normally just go out and buy your car – now might be the time to lease instead. Not only do you get the benefit of releasing cash but you also get the benefit of the greater buying power of the leasing companies. The driving force of leasing has, of course, always been tax. The leasing companies, which are normally subsidiaries of banks, are set up to be able to take maximum advantage of the tax benefits of leasing. Individual businesses that may not be paying tax or that will have to wait some time to realise tax write-offs often can't take the same advantage which is why, together with the other benefits, it may be better to lease than to buy.

There are two types of leasing for accounting purposes: the benefits of ownership accrue to the lessee when it is a finance lease, otherwise it is an operating lease. An example of an operating lease is a short-term lease on a property where the owner will get the asset back in, say, a year, but the lessee pays rent in the meantime. The accounting treatment of finance leasing is to look at the economic reality and treat it as if it were a purchase of the asset matched by a loan to pay for it. It does mean that banks and others will look at leasing as a form of borrowing when they review business accounts, which can limit how much leasing a business may want to do regardless of when leasing companies may feel enough is enough.

Other forms of finance

There are alternatives to bank finance but most of them are more appropriate to smaller businesses and start-ups than to substantial enterprises.

Friends and family

This is the classic funding route for most start-up businesses. One raises money from one's immediate circle either in the form of share capital or debt.

When setting up a new retail business, two out of the three founding directors were able to put in their own money. One was wealthy and could find a substantial sum, the second had a small amount of cash and was able to borrow some from his mother, and the third had no cash whatever and got just 'sweat equity', which is a term for being given shares in a business in recognition of work put in. The directors asked friends and family if they would invest and got 15 people to invest £300,000 in total alongside their own £300,000. Most of the investors had access to substantial funds but for several this was a significant investment.

Their investment was made through the UK government's Enterprise Investment Scheme (EIS), which gives tax benefits to

British taxpayers who invest in new shares in private companies. There are exclusions such as property companies and major shareholders, and the shares must generally be held for at least three years. The main benefits of the scheme are to allow the investor to offset the capital investment against his or her income tax liability and to be exempt from capital gains tax after three years. In the event, the business failed after 10 years but the investors were able to take advantage of a 'Negligible Value Claim' that allows investors to offset capital losses against income taxes that they have paid. EIS has since become less generous but higher rate taxpayers in this case will have offset their investment so that their losses will have been less that 40 per cent of their investment.

The use of outside shareholders increases the company secretarial workload since there is some effort involved in setting up an EIS, and there will need to be more detailed communication with shareholders than might be necessary if the shareholders were also working directors. Nonetheless the effort is not unreasonable. There may be a need for more detailed legal work to set up shareholder agreements or special share structures but this, also, is not massive.

It is usual to produce a business plan for any fundraising but, if possible, it is worthwhile taking steps to avoid having this classified as a 'prospectus'. There are special rules that apply to prospectuses, designed to protect less sophisticated investors from exploitation. In particular there is a requirement for an accountant's report and for due diligence, which can be expensive and push up the cost of any fundraising. There is also automatic responsibility for the contents of a prospectus that is shouldered by those issuing it, which is what gives rise to the need for due diligence which, in turn, demands the verification of the document, word by word, with all claims and data checked and justified.

To avoid having a business plan classed as a prospectus the document should be numbered and circulated to fewer than 50 people, it should not be made publicly available and there should be a form of words on the front cover that states it is not a prospectus. This should also make clear that no warranties are given and that recipients should satisfy themselves as to the accuracy of the content. It is probably worth getting a solicitor to provide wording consistent with the latest legislation.

Business angels

'Business angel' is a term used for an investor in a private company who is neither a friend nor family. Angels are individuals who seek profitable investments, who may seek a job in the company they invest in or who may want only limited involvement. There are a number of networks of such investors, often to be found through the internet or through firms of accountants.

Such investors will probably want specific protection if they are not involved in the business on a day-to-day basis. This will possibly limit the company's ability to borrow, to acquire or dispose of assets or parts of a business and to issue shares, as well as limiting transactions with directors and their remuneration. A business angel may also want to invest in a class of equity that confers preferential rights to dividends.

Venture capital

Venture capital is available from many investment groups but it must be borne in mind that few of these will provide smaller amounts of funding. Because the cost of assessing and managing a small investment is similar to that for a large investment, it is harder, in practice, to find venture capital investors for sums of less than £1 million.

The process of raising such funds may also be longer and more expensive than going through business angels. The venture capitalist will want to assess the proposition and then carry out due diligence to verify the information that has been supplied, which can involve an accountants' report and an industry expert's report. The company raising funds will be expected to pay for these. The process will include approval by an investment committee and will certainly take several weeks and can take several months.

If an investment proceeds then the venture capitalist will normally demand a seat on the board and special rights as outlined above for business angels. They will certainly require dividends each year and will probably have a target to realise their investment in three to five years, which may mean their agreement includes penalties, such as a higher share in the business, if this is not achieved. They would seek to realise their investment through a trade sale, merger or flotation, or by selling on some or all of their investment to another investor, which could be another venture capitalist.

Corporate venturing

Some large corporations invest in smaller companies to get access to their innovations. This is particularly true in high-tech industries but can also occur in more mundane areas such as restaurant chains where a larger company may want to develop new brands and concepts cheaply and can do so through taking a minority stake in a smaller business.

In most such cases the investing company will approach the 'target', but a business can seek out a partner to invest in it. It requires knowledge of one's marketplace and a willingness to approach possible investors, either directly or through an intermediary. It is even worthwhile considering possible partners who have not invested before if there seems to be a particularly good fit.

For an early stage or start-up business the management team would need evidence of an impressive track record with previous businesses or a particularly impressive idea. For an existing business, an excellent track record constrained only by a shortage of investment would be necessary.

In the UK there is a Corporate Venturing Scheme that offers to investing companies tax benefits similar to the private investors' EIS, such as a right to offset up to 20 per cent of an investment in new shares against corporation tax. There are conditions such as the investing company holding no more than 30 per cent of the share capital and not having management control. There are also detailed conditions for the investee company such as 20 per cent of the share capital being held by individuals other than directors or employees, and the company not being a subsidiary of another company.

Public fundraising

A very small number of companies will be suitable for raising money from the stock markets. In the UK, the largest of these is the London Stock Exchange. A listing on this is likely to cost over £1 million and companies must generally have a track record of at least five years.

The Exchange also oversees the smaller Alternative Investment Market, which has less onerous conditions for listing but costs to join will still be at least £500,000, which means that it will generally not be suitable for a company seeking to raise less than several million pounds, unless it is seeking a trading option for its shares rather than just fundraising.

London also has a successor to the old Ofex market for smaller companies, through Plus, which runs a primary market on a quote-driven basis, like the LSE and AIM, where a market-maker provides liquidity for trades. It also runs a secondary market on an order-driven basis, where parcels of shares are offered to traders and a trade only occurs if there is someone who expresses a wish to buy. Even this market, with its lower fees and easier entry requirements, will cost hundreds of thousands of pounds for a fundraising since there remains a requirement for an accountant's report to support a prospectus, legal and advisory fees.

Smaller companies must also be aware that liquidity in their shares will be limited on all these markets; they might find it difficult to sell shares when they want to because they cannot find a buyer on Plus, or because the desire to sell even a small parcel of shares leads to a massive drop in price on the other exchanges. The cost of membership of stock exchanges includes the necessary appointed advisers, annual fees, and levels of reporting that are not needed by private companies.

10

Company accounts

It is sometimes forgotten that company accounts serve two purposes; they are not just a legal requirement that has to be endured but are also an important form of communication with a variety of stakeholders in your business. We are all aware that accounts are used to communicate with shareholders and tax authorities, but they are also used with banks and credit agencies, suppliers and customers as well as potential business partners, or potential bidders for your business, even the trade press in your sector and, possibly, with employees. With some of these readers you will have some control over the presentation because you will send the accounts to them with a covering letter or commentary; with others, they will run a search on your accounts through Companies House (in the UK) and you will never know they have done so.

This wide usage of accounts suggests that businesses should try to present the picture they want to be out there. There are two ways of doing this; the first, which gives limited flexibility, is to use the choices available in picking accounting policies. For example, setting up a new retail business, we chose to write off the set-up costs quickly rather than using the available scope to capitalise costs and depreciate them gradually. We felt this communicated a conservative approach that would be more impressive to financial backers. The second way to influence the reader of accounts is through the commentary that accompanies them when sent for publication. Legal requirements are fairly limited but there is much to be said for doing more than the minimum. A longer, more detailed commentary could, for example, be sent to selected users such as shareholders. Also, many businesses – small companies as well as large – send a summary and explanation of financial information to employees. This can prove tricky if trading is poor because one wants to boost morale not depress it, but it is a potentially powerful tool if well handled.

Company structure

Different countries have different rules and types of company or partnership structures available. It is always worth checking from time to time whether your business has the appropriate structure, particularly in view of changing tax regimes. Take advice from professionals such as accountants; read what is available on the internet. Yesterday it may have been most tax-efficient to be a sole trader; today the limited company structure may be best; tomorrow it may be a limited partnership. Before making a change, always consider the wide range of non-financial issues too.

Someone who operated their business under a partnership decided to change that to a limited partnership structure for reasons that included image to clients, future succession planning and a small tax benefit. However, when it came to the final decision it was realised that the extra disclosure requirements of a limited partnership made it an unwise change. The financial sector they traded in put a premium on youth, partly because of the rapid changes in financial instruments and partly due to sheer prejudice. It was deemed unwise to have to disclose in filings that are publicly available that the businesses leaders were in their forties.

The cloak of limited liability is, of course, important in many cases.

Capital structure and risk

Is there an ideal capital structure that balances the correct level of debt and equity and, possibly, more obscure intermediate financing such as preference shares? I believe that for all practical purposes there is no answer to this. Companies are frequently urged by financiers to take on more debt, allowing them to pay some of this out to shareholders. The argument is that shareholders want a higher level of financial risk in their investment but I suspect the financiers are thinking of their fees.

The higher the level of debt that a business has, the higher its financial risk. It is easy to illustrate this. Consider a company that achieves sales of £1,000 and that has cost of sales at 50 per cent of sales, fixed costs at 20 per cent of sales and variable costs at 20 per cent of sales, leaving a contribution to profits of 10 per cent. Table 10.1 shows two alternative capital structures; the first has equity of £200, paying a dividend of 5 per cent and debt of £300, paying interest at 10 per cent; the second has equity of £500, paying a dividend of 5 per cent and no debt.

In this case, structure A provides shareholders who have £200 invested with a return of £120 (since they also own the retained profit) or 60 per cent, whilst structure B gives them £150 but it is only 30 per cent of their investment.

Imagine the business has an appalling year and sales drop by 30 per cent; this is shown in Table 10.2.

Table 10.1

Year	Structure A	Structure B
Sales	1,000	1,000
Cost of sales	500	500
Gross profit	**500**	**500**
Fixed costs	200	200
Variable costs	150	150
Profit before financing	**150**	**150**
Interest	30	0
Dividends	10	25
Retained profit	**110**	**125**

Table 10.2

Year	Company A	Company B
Sales	700	700
Cost of sales	350	350
Gross profit	**350**	**350**
Fixed costs	200	200
Variable costs	105	105
Profit before financing	**45**	**45**
Interest	30	0
Dividends	10	25
Retained profit	**5**	**20**

Structure A now only provides a return of 7.5 per cent whilst structure B provides 9 per cent. Moreover, in both cases the directors could decide not to pay dividends so as to conserve cash, but the effect is to give the company much more cash under structure B.

To audit or not to audit

In most countries it is a requirement to produce annual accounts for businesses in whatever form, if only for the calculation of tax. The rules for auditing such accounts vary greatly but the main factors are that it is usual for a lesser standard of disclosure to be demanded from smaller companies, and for smaller entities to be excused a full audit by outside accountants.

However, there are non-legal factors that should be considered. Banks and investors will often demand annual audited accounts, but whether you may seek outside finance in the future or want to sell the business, the people you speak to may demand to see audited accounts and you may be at a great disadvantage if you cannot provide them. On the other hand, clearly it saves a considerable amount of money not to have an audit. If your business is struggling you may want to save money and move to a lower, and cheaper, form of financial review, which may be sufficient. Whatever written agreements are in place, you may be able to get existing banks or investors to agree to vary them to excuse having to go through an audit.

The final consideration is your own peace of mind. You may prefer the reassurance that no significant accounting errors have been found. However good the accountant who produces internal company accounts, there will always be the possibility of error or being unaware of a problem that will benefit from external scrutiny. This is not to say that auditors are themselves infallible and will always spot errors or even fraud.

Early in my career I worked for a large company where I was assigned as acting finance director to a subsidiary that manufactured machine tools costing £1 million for the aerospace industry. The previous finance director, a respected, senior member of the accounting profession, had resigned suddenly after it was discovered he had borrowed money from the business. After a few weeks in my new role I noticed that heavy costs had been allocated to a machine that was under development and enquiries quickly revealed that this machine had not been ordered, was not assembled and was unlikely to be sold in its then current form. The account had simply been used to absorb £250,000 of costs that the previous management had not wanted to disclose in years when profits were low. Presumably they intended to release the costs in a year when profits were high. How did the auditors fail to notice high costs allocated to a machine in development for more than a year? This is not unusual: presumably the previous management wove a convincing story. Where incumbent management really understands their business they can often deflect auditors whose knowledge is more limited and who are only visiting for a short time.

Similar considerations to the audit question relate to publishing financial statements. Many countries require annual accounts of limited companies to be available for inspection, which is a great aid to credit reference agencies that analyse them. However, there are usually rules that allow limited disclosure for smaller companies; this allows you to keep information from competitors and also from those agencies. On the other hand, suppliers will often want to see a copy of your full disclosure accounts and may ask for them directly. On the whole I tend to think it is a good idea to volunteer full disclosure if you are confident in the future.

Accounting policies

Accounting standards require that accounting policies are disclosed with each set of published accounts, together with the bases of valuation and estimation. If accounting policies are changed, that must be declared and, as far as practicable, the effect that change would have had in the prior period must be shown, if it is material.

The list of policies that need to be disclosed is long; examples include:

- the length of time over which different asset classes are depreciated and the method used;
- whether interest is capitalised;
- how foreign currency transactions are converted;
- how intangible assets are treated;
- whether provisions are made for bad and doubtful debts and upon what basis;
- when different types of revenue are recognised.

Clearly the choice of accounting policy can have a material effect on the P&L a company publishes and can distort the apparent relative performance of different businesses within the same industrial sector.

Setting up a new business, I chose to depreciate computers over four years, in the face of our auditors' protest that three years was normal. In the event we used computers in the business for at least six years before changing them. However, my choice clearly reduced our depreciation charge and boosted our profits over the first three years. On the other hand, we decided to depreciate building works on our leased premises over eight years when our principle competitors chose 10 years.

Over the long term, the effects of such choices even out; the total depreciation charge is equal and the difference is one of timing. Suppose, for example, a single computer cost £1,200 then the two methods of depreciation would create the effect on P&L shown in Table 10.3.

Table 10.3

Year	1	2	3	4	5	6
3 yr	−400	−400	−400			
4 yr	−300	−300	−300	−300		

My choice of four-year depreciation boosted, for each computer, the P&L by £100 per year for three years, reduced it by £300 in the fourth year and we traded for a further two years with no charge.

These choices can have a significant effect in particular years and may affect the way stakeholders, whether shareholders, banks, prospective purchasers or business partners, see the business. It is important to think about the consequences in the light of future plans and choose carefully. If, for example, you expect to grow slowly for a few years then you may prefer to get costs out of the way early so that you can forecast higher profit later; on the other hand, if you expect rapid growth, it may be better to maximise short-term profits.

The acquisition of a business that has different accounting policies may provide an excuse to change and adopt them if they are more favourable. Without some 'cover' it can be hard to change established policies because of the need to show the effect in the previous year.

Issues of fraud

The question of fraud and its prevention is only peripherally related to that of auditing because there is no assurance that an audit will detect fraud. However, an outside audit does improve the chances of detection and also may highlight systemic weaknesses that can allow it to occur. There are straightforward precautions against fraud that should be in place that many organisations honour in their breach.

Satisfactory references should be a condition of employment, should always be requested from new employees and should always be taken up, ideally before they start work. This is even more important when the individual works in a role where they have access to cash or payments.

I worked for a company that did not take up references as a matter of course and only found it had taken on a convicted fraudster in its accounts department because someone who had known him from a previous employment, in a similar role, denounced him. She did so because his activities had driven that business into liquidation and she had lost her job as a result. The gap in our new employee's CV covered this employment and his subsequent prison term and really should have given rise to more searching questions.

Some employers will not supply references because they are fearful of the legal repercussions if unfavourable comments should become known to the employee. However, statements of fact cannot be actionable. It is important therefore to ask specific questions of fact such as dates of employment, whether the employee was honest and whether he or she left voluntarily. If previous employers will still not supply a reference, and some may only be willing to do so verbally, then one must take a view of the risks of offering employment. I would be very reluctant to do so in a finance role.

There should always be two signatories required on payments. Some web-based banking systems and Paypal make this hard to achieve, particularly in a small organisation, so there should be a process for such payments to be reviewed regularly by a second senior person. Look out for staff who don't take holidays or for sudden improvements in sales to occur when they do, or for co-signatories who seem too close. When finance staff are on holiday don't leave their work to await their return but have someone else cover it. Ideally use someone far more senior: coincidentally it is a great way to be sure you understand what is going on at the 'coal face'. This is the finance equivalent of the businesses that make senior executives work in their shops or restaurants for a period each year.

In a cash business it is very important to ensure that till discrepancies are reviewed and acted upon promptly. A small sum here or there can build up, over time, to be substantial. A pattern often emerges, with £10 disappearing every Thursday, for example. Extra observations can be used or a log taken of who operates which till and where the money disappears.

Trading ratios should be checked by unit as a matter of course. There was a case of a chef who stole meat. He was eventually caught because the ratio of food costs to sales seemed too high. If 'shrinkage' seems too high then maybe it is; a 'secret shopper' could be used to check that all transactions do indeed go through the till. In shops, pubs and clubs it is common for some staff to neglect to put some transactions through the till, as we know from our experience as customers. I constantly notice payments in shops and bars that don't seem to have gone through the till properly. If you are not handed a receipt then it has not gone through. Businesses should use anonymous visits to check on this.

There may be some readers who think I am devoting far too much space to this subject. I guess they don't appreciate how common theft is within the best organisations. Most is small scale and remains undiscovered, but it is a mistake to imagine it is irrelevant or that it is not there. I have come across it many times:

- **the finance director of an engineering company who borrowed money from the business;**
- **the salesman who shifted sales between months to ensure he got a bonus;**
- **the convicted fraudster who successfully got another finance job;**
- **the tills being short in shops and clubs and goods disappearing.**

Frauds and thefts are mostly simple and can be discouraged by strictly applying the obvious checks and balances such as:

- **dual signatures on cheques and set authorisation limits;**
- **receipts for expense claims;**
- **checks on new suppliers to ensure they exist;**
- **proper authorisation before paying invoices;**
- **proper authorisation of refunds;**
- **control of cheque books;**
- **examination of trading ratios and investigation of unusual discrepancies.**

Going concern

For directors whose businesses produce annual accounts and especially if you have an audit, it is necessary to consider each year whether the business is a going concern. If a business is struggling but not bankrupt, this can pose a significant problem because it requires the directors to make judgements based on information that may be uncertain. If a director can see that there is a significant risk that a business will need extra funding or will need to be sold, he or she has a duty to disclose this to the auditors. If the accounts are not audited, there may still be a duty to make disclosure in notes to the accounts.

Factors that may cast doubt on a going concern judgement:

- **the business has made either large trading losses or a series of trading losses over several years;**
- **the balance sheet shows a net liability;**
- **creditors cannot all be paid on time;**
- **loss of a key customer or supplier;**
- **withdrawal of credit or financial facilities.**

The factors to consider are the financial facilities: are they due for review or renewal? Will they be renewed? Will there be unacceptable conditions? Are you currently or likely to be in breach of any requirements? Review budgets and forecasts: are there significant adverse changes expected and what can be done about them?

This is quite a technical area where the law varies in detail from country to country and from time to time. However, the consequences of producing accounts that make no mention of a known problem can be significant. Creditors or banks that relied upon the accounts may be able to sue individual directors for compensation if the business fails. If you have any concerns, get professional advice.

The view when not a going concern

From an accounting point of view it is very rare to prepare accounts other than on a going concern basis, because if the company fails this test then it should not be trading. Sometimes, however, it may be helpful to prepare accounts on a break-up basis in order to understand what one's financial position is or to prepare a presentation to a rescuer or a bank. Bear in mind that almost all individual groups of assets are worth dramatically less in a break-up.

Fixed assets

Fixed assets such as property may be in the 'going concern' balance sheet at cost, although they may actually be worth more with the passage of time. However, leased property may be worth less because most leases provide for them to return to the landlord if the business fails (though administrators do have rights to assign leases, which partly offsets this). Plant and machinery, fixtures and fittings, computers and cars will often be worth far less in the second-hand market than even their depreciated value. Fitting out a bookstore, for example, cost over £50,000 to buy and install shelving whilst closing it and selling the same shelving only released £6,000. Cars will drop in value by 30 per cent the day you buy them; computers more than a year or two old are hard to sell at any price. Leased assets are worth nothing because they do not belong to the company. Intangible assets such as purchased goodwill will be worthless and intellectual property, including know-how and trademarks, may be hard to sell, rendering them also worthless.

Current assets

What about stocks? In a break-up these also tend to plummet in value. Given time to sell them, it may be possible to achieve the book value, but as a sale has to be achieved very quickly the stocks would have to be sold to 'dealers' and it is not unusual for stocks to be valued at just 10 per cent of book value with older, slower moving stocks even lower. Work in progress is, of course, valued at nothing unless there is an easy way of finishing the work. In some cases an administrator may continue to trade after being appointed, in the hope of achieving a sale as a going concern or to finish work-in-progress stocks so they can be sold. However, this requires a source of finance to be available, usually from the main creditors.

Debtors are also worth less in a break-up because there is a fear of counterclaims emerging or of customers taking advantage of the situation and being difficult, which adds cost to the collection process. Liabilities are valued the same in a going concern or break-up balance sheet.

Knowing that values plummet in a break-up does not stop one arguing for higher values as part of a presentation, but this will need justifying. Banks are well aware that when they are forced to take advantage of their security over assets, that security has a habit of evaporating. This is why business owners often feel aggrieved at the low valuation banks put on the assets offered to secure loans and why banks often seek personal guarantees from directors.

Trading whilst insolvent

In many countries directors who continue to trade while knowing their company is insolvent may face personal liabilities if it does become bankrupt. Creditors can take action to recover losses from the directors, who may also be barred from directorships of other companies. Such action by the authorities may affect the ability to raise personal credit since credit rating agencies become aware of it. It is usual for the liquidator to submit a report to the authorities and liabilities may arise in respect of transactions that occur up to several years before bankruptcy. Thus the transfer of assets to connected or even to unconnected parties may be looked into to make sure they were sold from the company at a fair value.

Surplus funds

For most businesses at most times it makes sense to keep spare cash working as hard as possible. This requires the constant review of cash forecasts and the transfer of surplus funds to interest-bearing accounts. When a company has larger sums to invest, perhaps because of seasonal inflows, it is possible to invest through banks' treasury operations at a higher rate of return than through normal deposit accounts. Often a slightly higher rate can be earned if funds are invested for a period such as a week or a month rather than on overnight call. However, it is important to be confident in one's cash forecast before tying money up in this way, as a small error for a few days can result in unnecessary interest costs that outweigh the benefits of many months of careful cash management.

There are times when one's main bank will pay lower rates of interest on deposits than other banks. It is always worthwhile checking market rates and considering placing a deposit with another bank, but it is equally important to be aware of the delay and the transaction fees that may arise in transferring funds from one to the other, which can outweigh the benefits.

At times when banks generally pay low rates of interest, investments in unusual instruments such as Premium Bonds (in the UK) suddenly look more attractive. You take the risk of earning nothing since this is gambling, but what the mathematical law of large numbers says is that the larger the number of gambles or, in this case, bonds, the greater the likelihood that your return will tend towards the average of some 3 per cent tax free. The investment is virtually risk free since it is made through a government institution and capital will not reduce in value. A business adviser told me he recommended this course to a client who invested £20,000 and promptly won £15,000. I fear that this does not mean that every investor will do as well!

In some countries at some times, when tax due is estimated it may be worthwhile overpaying because the authorities may pay an attractive rate of interest on monies that are returned. It is worth seeking advice on this if you have surplus funds.

11

Administration as a business tool

The process of administration is expensive but there may be circumstances when a business can be saved from complete failure by being put into administration and then buying out selected assets, cutting loose what you don't want. This can save jobs but the process is risky and should be carefully considered.

The administrators may be very helpful when you speak to them initially but once you appoint them you are in their hands and have no way of obliging them to keep to the deal you think you struck. They will sell the assets to the highest bidder and, if you want those assets, you must be the highest bidder. They may be slow to give you information you ask for.

Apart from the problems, outlined below, that relate to establishing a successor company there are immediate risks involved in putting a business into administration. For example, if the directors have continued to trade whilst the business was insolvent they could be personally liable for its debts – though there are excuses available, such as having a reasonable belief that an alternative solution would be found. Also, the administrators will look back over past transactions to ensure they were honest. There are also practical considerations such as the ability of the tax authorities to reclaim unpaid taxes from the directors in certain circumstances. In practice the authorities will not do this if the directors have behaved properly, but it can be a worry.

Administration issues
Retention of title

In many countries suppliers will try to retain the legal ownership of goods until they have been paid for, which means that if a company becomes insolvent the supplier can reclaim the goods. Indeed they may well try to reclaim the goods before insolvency is declared. How successful this process is depends upon the laws of each country. This procedure seems to be common in Europe and particularly in Germany and the UK, but while it exists in the United States, it seems to be less popular, perhaps because of the stay on bankruptcy proceedings that follow from its Chapter 11 insolvency.

In the UK this contract clause is often called the 'Romalpa clause' after a seminal early case. There are two stages to implementing it: first to show that title was retained at the time of the original contract; secondly that the goods can be identified. It is common to get the customer to sign the terms and conditions of the supplier, which will include this clause – this achieves the first stage. Alternatively, the terms and conditions of sale, including retention of legal title to goods, may be printed on the back of each invoice. The terms and conditions may demand that goods are segregated from other suppliers', goods which may be more or less practical. The process often falls down when it comes to identifying goods, which may come from several sources and may not be segregated or easily identified in practice: it then comes down to negotiation or rejection of the claim by the insolvency practitioner. If you want to take advantage of the clause then it is a good idea to check that your goods are identifiable, whilst if you want to frustrate it, your interests are to mix goods so that it is hard to identify their origins.

Voluntary arrangement

Some countries, such as the UK, have a procedure that is an alternative to bankruptcy where it can be shown that a business is viable but has temporary cash flow problems. In these circumstances it is often possible to reach an agreement with creditors so that the business continues to trade but pays either only a proportion of the debts due or else pays over a period of time – or both these things. The procedure may be managed by the courts or by business recovery experts, which adds cost to the procedure but the directors of the business stay in control. It is normal for the scheme to require a recovery plan to be put to creditors, a specified majority of whom, by value, have to approve it for it to go into effect. Of course the secured creditors, such as banks and landlords, will be in a position to demand full repayment if their security remains valid. After the process is complete the business resumes its normal trading under the control of the same directors and shareholders.

Informal arrangements may also be possible if creditors trust the management and can see that the company is able to trade its way out of difficulty. This may be a preferable alternative to allowing a customer to become insolvent.

The pre-pack

A special case of the administration process has been devised in an effort to try to keep businesses trading after a bankruptcy, even if it means selling it back to its original owners. This is called a 'pre-pack', or pre-packaged process. Essentially it means that the business is prepared, even before it goes into administration. The owners or others prepare an offer in advance for the assets they want and make it immediately and conditional on a quick sale – which usually takes place within hours. The justification for a pre-pack is that it preserves the maximum value for creditors by preventing the business losing value during a protracted administration. This loss in value may arise from factors such as losing customers if a business cannot obtain stocks to continue trading, or from losing critical staff who find other jobs. It can be put through without the consent of unsecured creditors but will still require the agreement of the secured creditors such as banks. The creditors have some protection because the administrator must be able to show they have behaved properly and justify their actions.

The other disadvantage of administration is that, as a director of a company in administration, your personal credit rating is adversely affected immediately. If you personally or a new company you set up and of which you are a director try to apply for a credit account, you will find there is a problem within a day or two of your original company going into administration. This applies not just to you but also to other people living at your address, so nominating your spouse as a director of the new company may not help. If, for example, you need an account with Royal Mail in order to trade, get this set up in the new business before the original business is put into administration. You may think that suppliers will simply be tougher on their credit terms – you would be wrong: they may refuse supply completely or demand a substantial up-front deposit. Some suppliers who use trade indemnity insurance may face difficulties supplying a successor company, regardless of whether or not they have lost money and even if they want to continue trading, if their insurers will not cover a successor company.

We put our bookselling business into administration but were keen to pay all creditors and for its successor company to continue trading with the main distributors. We offered to pay each creditor of the old company if they would agree to supply the new one on the same terms. One of the biggest suppliers was keen to transfer trading to the new company but its insurers would not agree. This meant that we did not pay them more than

£20,000 of debts in the old company and we had to buy the goods we wanted through a wholesaler.

Another problem for a successor company is that banks are reluctant to provide banking facilities, even if the bank that served the old company has not lost any money and even if the new company is not seeking a borrowing facility. If you persevere and tell a convincing story, you may find a bank that will agree to provide a current account, but it's hard work. Even once you have obtained banking facilities you may still have problems with elements you would regard as a normal part of banking. For example, the bank will view paying staff electronically through BACS as a borrowing requirement and may be unwilling to provide it to a successor company. There are less convenient alternatives, such as paying staff through internet accounts, but they seldom link in to payroll bureaux.

Precautions

It makes sense to set up a new company and get its credit accounts and banking established before putting the old one into administration. This may not be easy if you reluctantly decide upon administration as a last resort and at the last moment. Unfortunately you must take a precautionary approach and it is better to have your successor company established even if you do not need to use it in the end. Don't worry about being embarrassed: that is better than the host of other problems that may assail you. Maybe go to a different bank for facilities, perhaps establish some trading with suppliers so that you have some accounts opened – they will often be difficult about opening accounts after a bankruptcy but will seldom close existing ones. Think about who your key suppliers are. They are not just the people who supply stock; the telephone companies are critical: if they won't transfer telephone lines to a successor company then you may have a problem. Post, courier and utility companies are also critical.

Property

Consider property issues carefully before turning to administration. Most leases revert to the landlord in an administration. Of course if that was always enforceable, companies going into administration could never be saved. In fact the administrator can go to court to overturn or delay application of this clause, but the landlord may be able to get a large up-front deposit or directors' guarantees to support a transfer to a new lessor. You may be able to speak to your landlord before administration occurs and they may be willing to give an informal indication of their intentions. However, they may be reluctant to say too much for fear of being accused of having encouraged the administration. If you make an offer to buy the business from administration then you can make it conditional upon the transfer of leases.

So, if there are all these actual and potential problems, why use administration as a business tool? The answer is that it is worthwhile if you have no practical alternative, if a part of the business is dragging the rest down or if you can restructure the business at a lower cost base.

Starting again

If you see no choice but to start again with a new business then the issues highlighted above apply. This is an argument, also, in favour of trying your utmost to put any new business areas during the normal course of trading into new companies rather than an existing company. You often, for example, find that small restaurant and hotel chains have each operation owned by a separate company. If any chain becomes large this process becomes redundant because banks and suppliers who are supplying them all will seek guarantees between sister companies.

If following this scheme you do have to be careful about the share ownership of different companies to ensure you are not disadvantaging or even defrauding shareholders in any one company by excluding them from another or by transferring assets, which can include a trading name or intellectual property, into another company.

After the failure of a business you may not be able to use the same or a very similar name. In the UK while one can buy a trading name from an administrator, if the same directors are involved in both companies it is necessary to inform creditors of what is happening. They may have the right to protest and it may be possible for them to block the use of an old trading name. In other countries use of the old name may be banned outright.

An administrator of a failed business must report on the conduct of its directors to the UK authorities, which can lead to their being banned from being directors of another company if misconduct is proved. This extends to a person acting as a 'shadow director', which is someone acting as a director without formally being appointed as such. Any person who acts as a shadow director is always liable in exactly the same circumstances as one who is properly appointed.

12

Use all those free resources

Discounts and grants

We should all search out free resources at all times and take advantage of what is on offer. Many trade associations offer discounted attendance for 'first timers' at trade shows. Exporting businesses may be eligible for government assistance with travel or other costs to attend sales events overseas. There are often government-funded initiatives for particular industries or particular regions. For example, development grants are often available for deprived areas or old coal mining areas, perhaps through the EU, national or local government. In the UK there is a government-sponsored organisation called Business Link, with its own website, that supports smaller businesses. There are also commercial resources such as the www.is4profit.com website. Search the internet – ask people – there are lots out there and often similar schemes in countries outside the UK.

The UK government, for example, claims to administer a wide variety of schemes providing some £5 billion per annum to businesses through:

- grants – though these are usually on a matching basis, up to 50 per cent of project requirements;
- subsidised training;
- free or subsidised consultancy;
- soft loans, etc.

These schemes will depend upon: location, such as in a designated area in need of development; size, invariably applying to smaller businesses; and industry, either excluding some industries or applying solely to industries with recognised problems.

In the UK there is also the government's Small Firms Loan Guarantee Scheme that helps businesses that do not have assets to offer as security for loans. This is administered by the lending banks and guarantees 75 per cent of loans up to £250,000, though the average was just under £80,000 in 2007 across over 2,700 businesses. The borrower has to pay an extra 2 per cent interest for the guarantee. This encourages banks to invest in businesses where they would otherwise feel the risk was too high for them.

Reclaim taxes

Are you reclaiming all those tax rebates you are entitled to?

If you have paid foreign VAT on goods and services then you may be unable to reclaim it through your domestic returns but may be entitled to reclaim it directly. Which VAT on expenses is covered varies from country to country but can cover hotel accommodation, car rental, marketing costs, some professional services, etc. For some businesses these can be substantial sums and, although the process can be difficult, it is worth pursuing. From 1 January 2010 each EU country should provide an online gateway for its registered VAT businesses to make claims throughout the EU. Further information should be found from your own authority if you are registered for VAT within the EU; in the UK HMRC provides information on http://www.hmrc.gov.uk/vat/managing/international/overseas-traders.htm.

If, unfortunately, you have been associated with a business that has failed you may be able to reclaim a part, at least, of your losses. The way this works is that if you invested money in the shares of an unquoted company and those shares are now worthless, you can make a claim to your tax office to offset your loss against income taxes you have paid rather than just against capital gains tax profits. This enables you to get the money back much faster and means the opportunity is not lost if you have no capital gains to offset. You just write a letter citing a 'Section 574 Negligible Value Claim'; this is section 574 of the Income and Corporation Taxes Act 1988. Clearly you must be able to prove that the shares are now worthless and you really need to show that the company is in administration or being liquidated, but if you can prove it is no longer trading and is dormant then that may be sufficient. Although many accountants will offer to submit such claims for a percentage of the money they recover, in fact you ought to be able to do this yourself: it is not hard. Just write a letter to your HMRC office making the claim and explaining it is a Section 574 claim. You will need to specify which tax year you want to offset the claim against and you can use either the current year or carry it back up to two years. Carrying the claim back has the advantage of getting the money back more quickly. Also choose the year where you paid most tax at the highest rate. If there is not enough tax to offset in any year then you can offset against each of the two years available for carry-back.

Paying taxes

If cash is tight and you have a significant tax bill coming up, there may be scope to delay the payment or spread it out over several months. This may require you to pay interest and the authorities may want to be reassured that the problem is temporary and that you will be able to pay over a short period.

It is also worth checking with your tax adviser to see whether more recent losses can be used to offset a past tax liability before you have to pay it. Can your tax year-end be changed to achieve this?